Don't Take Away My Adderall!

The Unintended Consequences of Stimulant Prescription

Wayne Lewis Creelman, MD
Sang-Wahn Koo, MD
William Yvorchuk, MD

(University of Florida Department of Psychiatry,
Vero Beach Center)

Disclaimer

Several brand-name medications are used in this text, sometimes interchangeably with their generic equivalents. For appropriate credit the brand name medication and its registered trademark pharmaceutical company are listed here for the reader's knowledge, information, and benefit:

1. Shire: Adderall®, Vyvanse®, Daytrana®, Intuniv®
2. Novartis: Ritalin®, Methylphenidate®, Focalin®
3. Abbott: Cylert®, Dexedrine®
4. Janssen: Concerta®
5. Smith, Kline, and French: Benzedrine®
6. Lily: Strattera®, Prozac®
7. Teva: Modafinil®
8. Concordia: Kapvay®

The information provided in this text is for educational purposes only, is the expressed opinion of the authors, and does not substitute for professional medical advice. Please consult a medical professional or healthcare provider for medical advice, diagnosis, or treatment.

First Printing – February 2023

Digital Publishing of Florida, Inc.
Oldsmar, FL 34677
www.digitaldata-corp.com

Proudly Printed in the United States of America

Table of Contents

Introduction

This book focuses our attention on one popular movement in recent years, namely the ever-increasing demand for stimulants for emotional wellbeing and performance enhancement. Whereas, the paradoxical response to stimulants in children with true ADHD which is thought to be protective against misuse, the regular ingestion of substances like Adderall® in normal individuals can lead to abuse and life-threatening complications particularly in our older population.

Drs. Creelman, Koo and Yvorchuk are active clinicians caring for patients on a daily basis and members of the faculty of the University of Florida College of Medicine. This text contains a discussion of the gross over-expansion of diagnosing the problem of ADHD, the unintended consequences of over-diagnosing and over-prescribing for the condition as well as viable solutions for the population that is currently being harmed.

1

Do We Have a Problem?

(Wayne Lewis Creelman, MD)

As a practicing psychiatrist and psychopharmacologist along with two of my colleagues - a child psychiatrist and an addictionologist, we have come to the realization that an unfortunate phenomenon is taking place in American medicine. More particularly, in the field of psychiatric and addiction medicine. The American public is well acquainted with the phenomenon of attention deficit disorder or now more commonly referred to as attention deficit hyperactivity disorder, ADHD, this label for both children and adults has become a clinical problem.

When this phenomenon was first recognized in children the term minimal brain dysfunction was used, however now this term has evolved into the current ADHD. For many years the medication Ritalin was used to treat this pathology, now Adderall and amphetamine derivatives are the more common options. Earlier in my career as a practicing psychiatrist, magnesium pemoline (Cylert) was a very effective medication for assisting with focus, concentration skills, retention of information and task completion but it was taken off the market as a consequence of liver damage and is no longer available for prescription.

Unfortunately, the ADHD medications today are being as over prescribed as are antibiotics. This is not a benign

1

situation. Of all of the many available anti-ADHD medications that are used, the majority can become highly addictive over time. One exception is Strattera (atomoxetine) which is typically prescribed as a first line treatment for symptoms associated with ADHD but unfortunately has not proven to be as effective as Adderall or Concerta. The newest kid on the block so to speak is Vyvanse which was launched in July of 2008 by Shier pharmaceuticals. Today Johnson and Johnson is the pharmaceutical company pushing the use of Concerta. As a consequence, the current treatment and state of over diagnosing ADHD has become a national disaster of dangerous proportions.

The problem we have before us is that the reality of the situation is that amphetamines and amphetamine derivatives can basically help anyone. They are especially helpful in individuals whose jobs require high levels of concentration and or stamina. It is well-known that workplace productivity was boosted enormously back in the 1930's with the introduction of Benzedrine. The problem that has arisen are the excessive and outrageous rates of ADHD diagnoses that are being made by the medical community in the USA. This is both a good news and bad news scenario.

To some extent the good news involves the fact that family practitioners and primary care physicians, as well as internal medicine specialists, very often refuse to prescribe any controlled substances including the amphetamines and amphetamine-like derivatives for treatment of ADHD. They will send their patients to the local psychiatrist or mental health physician assistant or nurse practitioner to prescribe these medications. As a consequence, the patient presents at the office of a mental health practitioner with the assumption that they will leave with a prescription for one of the stimulant medications to improve their lifestyle success. As was mentioned above, basically anyone using these medications will like how they make them feel, be happy at the increase in stamina experienced and be pleased at the results that personal achievement rewards.

Recognizing that the use of psychostimulants has been a godsend for children, as well as young men and women suffering attention deficit hyperactivity disorder, allowing them to successfully overcome deficits of being able to focus effectively, comprehend material quickly and succeed in task completion, a new unintended consequence has occurred. The misuse and overuse of ADHD medication, especially in the high school and college student body is widespread. Approximately 1,000,000 high school youngsters nationwide in the United States use either Adderall, Concerta or Vyvanse without a physician's prescription as they get the medication from friends or dealers at $2 a pill. They also receive prescriptions from physicians under faults pretenses. The ability to complete self-rating scales to warrant a prescription is widespread, regardless of the absence of any true ADHD symptoms. A typical college student will tell you that "if I had Adderall's energy running through my veins with caffeine anything would be possible." Unfortunately, a user of these medications can become dependent overtime on these drugs relating to both their physical and psychological effects, even when the medications are used for legitimate purposes.

It is estimated that 1/500 youngsters experience hallucinations while on these medications and with over

500,000 people starting ADHD meds every year in the USA, statistically, approximately 1000 will experience hallucinations of a frightening and debilitating nature. On occasion these medications also will cause amphetamine psychoses as college students typically double or triple doses for increased stamina and productivity. More recently the ADHD meds have been used to assist with eating disorders by suppressing appetite, especially with young women obsessed with a distorted body image and the "thin is in" culture promoted by many media outlets as well as social media applications.

Some estimates indicate that 1/10 of individuals who utilize stimulants improperly became addicted to these medications at some level. The number of people entering drug rehabilitation programs for abuse of Adderall and other stimulants has risen dramatically over the last 10 years. These unintended consequences raise the importance of making an accurate diagnosis and closely following individuals prescribed with these medications over extended periods of the life cycle.

It has come to our attention during our clinical work that there exists a gray zone between the time that attention deficit disorder pathology ends and the addiction to these amphetamine-like medications begins, thus placing many individuals at risk for amphetamine addiction, intoxication and negative medical consequences. For example, the Connor's scale has 28 questions that are answered by the test-taker with 0-3 answers for all questions. This rating scale is very easy to fake if one is interested in obtaining ADHD medications. Another problem is that the diagnosis of ADHD often times is handled recklessly by medical doctors with quick 5 to 10-minute evaluations and then a prescription is being generated to the drug seeker. Many of the screening tools for ADHD are simply a series of between 6 and 18 bogus questions with the results that favorable responses whether accurate or not will generate the working diagnosis of ADHD. When one looks at the problem it is sometimes difficult to distinguish between the bigger problem, dishonest patients versus lazy doctors.

The over prescription of ADHD medications and abuse of these medications have recently caused shortages in pharmacies as the pharmaceutical companies cannot manufacture these medications fast enough to satisfy the nationwide craving. Many patients are seen by very casual and disinterested physicians or clinicians who bypass the child or adult's real problems or unfortunately yield to the frustrated parents and teachers with out-of-control classrooms and blame the problem on ADHD untreated children.

The field has even suggested a precursor to ADHD called SCT, slowed cognitive tempo, which in some circles is begging to be made official in order to start youngsters on these medications earlier in their academic careers. The reality is that pediatricians and primary care physicians simply do not have the training to prescribe these medications for legitimate ADHD youngsters but they do anyway. Often times when a history of procrastination is mentioned by a child or parent, the diagnosis of ADHD is made on the spot. Indeed, there are individuals who truly meet the criteria and warrant a diagnosis however many do not satisfy criteria but get the diagnosis anyway and the prescription.

The purpose of this expose is to review the indications for the use of psychostimulant medication, address the overuse of these medications in the United States and the consequences, as opposed to the rest of the globe and then how to convince adults that they are not in need of the continued use of these medications lifelong. Unfortunately, as children are growing up both with the legitimate diagnoses of ADHD as well as those individuals who have feigned symptoms to obtain stimulant medication, Big Pharma wants to keep their business. The pharmaceutical industry has made it extremely user friendly to purchase their products. Shire pharmaceuticals has a toll-free number (1- 888-ASK-ADHD) to diagnosis yourself after answering 6 questions. In reality, the majority of legitimate ADHD children do not retain symptoms past childhood. The best estimates suggest that possibly 4.4 percent of American adults have residual ADHD, resulting in approximately 10,000,000 purchased prescriptions of stimulant medication.

The literature is essentially absent regarding any recognition or acknowledgement that stimulants have a high abuse potential and are addictive, especially in the adult population. The growth of the stimulant medication market has been astronomical. Estimates for prescriptions for ADHD in 2007 were within the ballpark of 5.6 million while 5 years later almost 16,000,000 were written, almost tripling the numbers. It is clear from our clinical work that many adults simply using amphetamine derivatives as performance enhancing drugs. Today the population of American adults taking ADHD drugs with no clear diagnosis of the pathology is moving past 5,000,000 users with the numbers increasing every year. Vyvanse has a new IND (official indication) for binge eating disorder that will generate for Shire pharmaceuticals over 2 billion dollars this year. This Pharma giant is beginning to worry as the patent on Vyvanse expires in 2023, when generic knockoffs will remove their market share.

The adult population is clearly becoming the new ADHD growth market. Other countries do not appear to be over diagnosing ADHD as is the United States based on parental impatience or corporate greed. In particular, Brazil, France, Italy and Sweden are very conservative regarding making the ADHD diagnosis and at one point in time, Canada, Italy and Sweden have actually banned stimulant medications. It should be no surprise that in United States, the prescriptions for amphetamines and Ritalin stimulants are over 90 percent of the world's total usage. It is nothing short of shocking that 10,000 toddlers, ages 2 and 3 who are still in diapers are being prescribed Adderall and Concerta to give them a jump on academic competitiveness. The reality is that the diagnosis of ADHD should be in the ballpark of about 5 percent in children and no more than 2.5 percent of the adult population. The bottom line however is that ADHD is here to stay and the challenge for the future will be accurate diagnoses, appropriate medication intervention and very close oversight of dosage and duration of treatment.

This book in essence is a public health announcement. However, no public health announcement would be credible unless those individuals making a claim were not also credible themselves. The three physician authors of this text have a combined total of more than 80 years of clinical experience in the daily treatment of children, adolescents and adults suffering ADHD.

Dr. Creelman is the McCabe Professor of Psychiatry at the University of Florida, board-certified in general psychiatry and a national expert in community psychiatry and psychopharmacology. He trained at Boston College, Georgetown School of Medicine and Tulane School of Public Health.

Dr. Sang Koo is an assistant professor of psychiatry at the University of Florida Department of Psychiatry, board-certified in child and adult psychiatry and completed a prestigious fellowship in Child and Adolescent Psychiatry at the Washington University School of Medicine in Saint Louis Missouri.

Dr. William Yvorchuk is an assistant professor in the Department of Psychiatry at the University of Florida, the medical director of Addiction Medicine at the Vero Beach Center for Psychiatry and Addiction Medicine, completed a fellowship in Addiction Medicine at the University of Florida College of Medicine and is certified in Addiction Medicine by the American Board of addiction medicine. He is also a diplomate of the American Board of Preventive Medicine.

All three are active clinicians caring for patients on a daily basis and members of the faculty of the University of Florida College of Medicine.

What follows is an expansion of the problem of ADHD, the unintended consequences of over diagnosing and overprescribing treatment as well as viable solutions for the population that is being harmed.

2

Opinions Based on Facts and Concerns of Adderall Use in Pediatric Population in the US

(Sang-Wahn Koo, MD)

"Moreover, my marriage is falling apart because of Anthony. He puts a lot of strain on the relationship with my husband."

Parents brought their 12-year-old Anthony to a local emergency department (ED) with complaints of irritability. They say he went from "zero to sixty" and began screaming, throwing objects, threatening parents, and pounding their bedroom walls when a limit was set on his electronic tablet access. In the ED, he is calm and cooperative, and parents report a typically "happy go lucky child." These outbursts, occurring a few times a month, resolve within a few hours and are frequently triggered by Anthony not "getting his way."

I see children and adolescents as well as adults with mental health conditions in the University of Florida Center for Psychiatry and Addiction Medicine, Vero Beach clinic in Vero Beach, Florida. A significant proportion of the children and adolescents that I see in the clinic present with either attention-deficit/hyperactivity disorder (ADHD) or ADHD with oppositional defiant disorder (ODD). The description above is most consistent with attention-deficit/hyperactivity disorder (ADHD) with oppositional defiant disorder (ODD) (Carlson & Klein, 2020).

What is ADHD?

Attention-deficit/hyperactivity disorder (ADHD) is a neurodevelopmental disorder and one of the most common neurobehavioral disorders of childhood and can profoundly affect children's academic achievement, well-being, and social interactions (Wolraich et al., 2019). Since it is a neurodevelopmental disorder, it is hard to imagine for an adult to develop this syndrome de novo when he is in his 30's or 40's let alone in his 50's and 60's. Based on the literature, up to 60% of children continue to exhibit the ADHD symptoms even though they reach adulthood (Biederman et al., 2000; Kessler et al., 2005).

Symptoms of ADHD include those related to inattention and/or hyperactivity and impulsivity. Youth with ADHD often have difficulty paying close attention to details, are reluctant to engage in tasks requiring sustained attention, or may experience difficulty with impulse control such as leaving their seat when sitting is expected, or speaking out of turn excessively (Amerian Psychiatric Association, 2013). In order for a diagnosis of ADHD to be made, the behaviors and symptoms may not solely be a manifestation of oppositional behavior, defiance, hostility, or failure to understand tasks or instructions (Amerian Psychiatric Association, 2013).

The DSM (Diagnostic and Statistical Manual of Mental Disorders)-5 system is used by professionals in psychiatry, psychology, health care systems, and primary care; it is also well established with third-party payers (Amerian Psychiatric Association, 2013). The DSM-5 diagnostic criteria for ADHD are as follows (Amerian Psychiatric Association, 2013):

A. A persistent pattern of inattention and/or hyperactivity-impulsivity that interferes with functioning or development, as characterized by (1) and/or (2):

1. **Inattention:** Six (or more) of the following symptoms have persisted for at least 6 months to a degree that is inconsistent with developmental level and that negatively impacts directly on social and academic/occupational activities: **Note:** Those symptoms are not solely a manifestation of oppositional behavior, defense, hostility, or failure to understand tasks or instructions. For older adolescents and adults (age 17 and older), at least five symptoms are required.

a. Open fails to give close attention to details or makes careless mistakes in schoolwork, at work, or during other activities (e.g., overlooks or misses details, work is inaccurate).

b. Often has difficulty sustaining attention in tasks or play activities (e.g., has difficulty remaining focused during lectures, conversations, or lengthy reading).

c. Often does not seem to listen when spoken to directly (e.g., mind seems elsewhere, even in the absence of any obvious distraction).

d. Often does not follow through on instructions and fails to finish schoolwork, chores, or duties in the workplace (e.g., starts tasks but quickly loses focus and is easily sidetracked).

e. Often has difficulty organizing tasks and activities (e.g., difficulty managing sequential tasks; difficulty keeping materials and belongings in order; messy, disorganized work; has poor time management; fails to meet deadlines).

f. Often avoids, dislikes, or is reluctant to engage in tasks that require sustained mental effort (e.g., schoolwork or homework; for older adolescents and adults, preparing reports, completing forms, reviewing lengthy papers).

g. Often loses things necessary for tasks or activities (e.g., school materials, pencils, books, tools, wallets, keys, paperwork, eyeglasses, mobile telephones).

h. Is often easily distracted by extraneous stimuli (for older adolescents and adults, may include unrelated thoughts).

i. Is often forgetful in daily activities (e.g., doing chores, running errands; for older adolescents and adults, returning calls, paying bills, keeping appointments).

2. **Hyperactivity and impulsivity**: Six (or more) of the following symptoms have persisted for at least 6 months to a degree that is inconsistent with developmental level and that negatively impacts directly on social and academic/occupational activities: **Note:** The symptoms are not solely a manifestation of oppositional behavior, defiance, hostility, or failure to understand tasks or instructions. For older adolescents and adults (age 17 or and older), at least five symptoms are required.

a. Often fidgets with or taps hands or feet or squirms in seat.
b. Often leaves seat in situations when remaining seated is expected (e.g., leaves his or her place in the classroom, in the office or other workplace, or in other situations that require remaining in place).
c. Often runs about or climbs in situations where it is inappropriate. (**Note:** In adolescents or adults, may be limited to feeling restless.)
d. Often unable to play or engage in leisure activities quietly.
e. Is often "on the go," acting as if "driven by a motor" (e.g., is unable to be or uncomfortable being still for extended time, as in restaurants, meetings; may be experienced by others as being restless or difficult to keep up with).
f. Often talks excessively.
g. Often blurts out an answer before a question has been completed (e.g., completes people's sentences; cannot wait for turn in conversation).
h. Often has difficulty waiting his or her turn (e.g., while waiting in line).
i. Often interrupts or intrudes on others (e.g., butts into conversations, games, or activities; may start using other people's things without asking or receiving permission; for adolescents and adults, may intrude into or take over while others are doing).

B. Several inattentive or hyperactive-impulsive symptoms were present prior to age 12 years.

C. Several inattentive or hyperactive-impulsive symptoms are present in two or more settings (e.g., at home, school, or work; with friends or relatives; in other activities).

D. There is clear evidence that the symptoms interfere with, or reduce the quality of, social, academic, or occupational functioning.

E. Those symptoms do not occur exclusively during the course of schizophrenia or another psychotic disorder and are not better explained by another mental disorder (e.g., mood disorder, anxiety disorder, dissociative disorder, personality disorder, substance intoxication or withdrawal).

The DSM-5 criteria define 3 dimensions of ADHD (American Psychiatric Association, 2013):

314.01 (F90.2) Combined presentation: If both Criterion A1 (inattention) and Criterion A2 (hyperactivity-impulsivity) are met for the past six months.

314.00 (F90.0) Predominantly inattentive presentation: If Criterion A1 (inattention) is met but Crierion A2 (hyperactivity-impulsivity) is not met for the past six months.

314.01 (F90.1) Predominantly hyperactive/impulsive presentation: If Criterion A2 (hyperactivity-impulsivity) is met and Criterion A1 (inattention) is not met for the past six months.

The History of ADHD

The syndrome of ADHD was first described by a German physician in 1775 (Barkley & Peters, 2012; Faraone et al., 2015). In 1937, the efficacy of amphetamine use to reduce symptom severity was serendipitously discovered (Faraone et al., 2015). In the 1940s. the brain was implicated as the source of ADHD-like symptoms, which were described as minimal brain damage in the wake of an encephalitis epidemic (Faraone et al., 2015). The first diagnosis to describe children with symptoms of ADHD was the diagnosis of Hyperkinetic Impulse Disorder introduced by Laufer et al (1957). In 1970 the second edition of the *Diagnostic and Statistical Manual of Mental Disorders* (DSM) (Amerian Psychiatric Association, c1970) identified the syndrome as "hyperkinetic reaction" based on the then-prevailing psychodynamic philosophy that mental disorders were always reactions to some stressor (Spetie & Arnold, 2018). As one may be familiar with the name Freud, he is regarded as the founding father of psychoanalysis and psychodynamic philosophy originated from his theories. Freud chose the word "analysis" to suggest analogy to work done by chemists, who isolate fundamental substances, that is, chemical elements, in their laboratories (Karasu, 2017). In 1980, the third edition of the *Diagnostic and Statistical Manual of Mental Disorders* (DSM) (Amerian Psychiatric Association, c1980) created the first reliable operational diagnostic criteria for the disorder (Faraone et al., 2015). DSM-III-R(revised) (Amerian Psychiatric Association, c1987) added overactivity back to the name of the disorder via the term "attention-deficit/hyperactivity disorder (ADHD) (Spetie & Arnold, 2018). This name was retained by DSM-IV although the symptom list changed somewhat, being expanded from 14 to 18 symptoms and being split into two lists of nine each (Spetie & Arnold, 2018). The age requirement for symptom onset was changed age 12 in the DSM-5 (rather than age 7 in DSM-IV), but the name of the disorder was preserved as in DSM-III-R (Spetie & Arnold, 2018).

Figure 1. The history of attention-deficit/hyperactivity disorder.

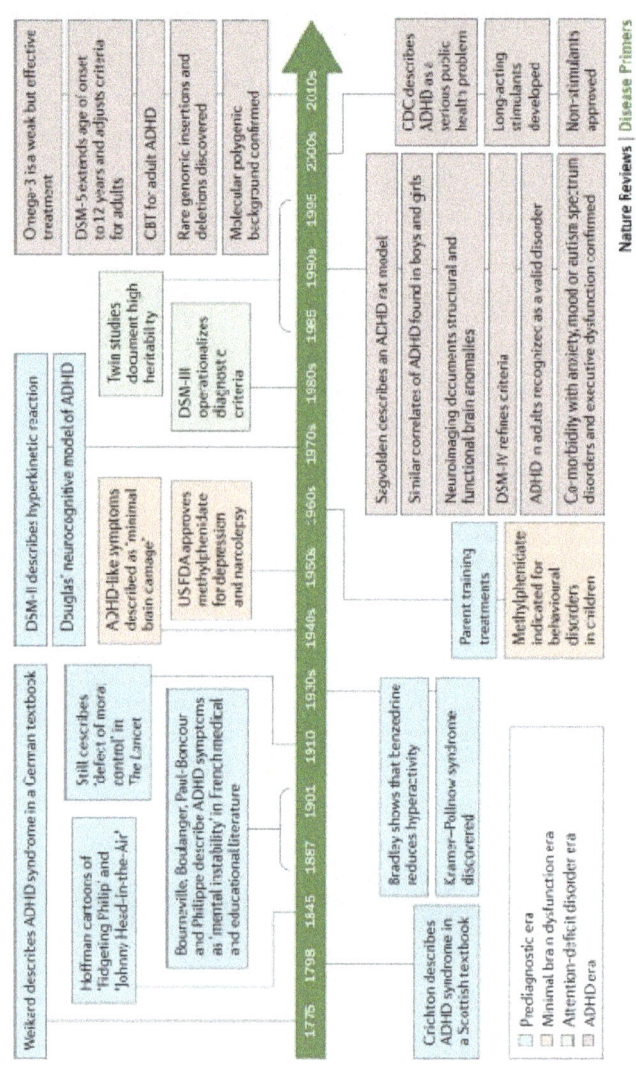

The history of attention-deficit/hyperactivity disorder
(Faraone et al., 2015)

How prevalent is ADHD?

A useful measure to quantify the occurrence of a specific condition in a population is the prevalence estimate, a ratio describing the number of people with a disorder in a specific population in a designated time period (Sadock et al., 2017). Prevalence estimates of ADHD vary on the basis of differences in research methodologies, the various age groups being described, and changes in diagnostic criteria over time (Holbrook et al., 2017). The increasing rates and the geographic variation in the prevalence of ADHD have generated controversy about the basis of clinical diagnosis and treatment of the disorder (Hinshaw & Scheffler, 2014; Mayes et al., 2008; Schwarz, 2016).

Population surveys suggest that ADHD occurs in most cultures in about 5% of children and about 2.5% of adults (Amerian Psychiatric Association, 2013). However, one study of 842,830 children treated between the years of 2001 and 2010 found that in 2010, the prevalence of ADHD among non-Hispanic white children was 5.6%, whereas the prevalence among African American youth and Hispanic youth was 4.1% and 2.5%, respectively (Getahun et al., 2013).

National survey data from 2016 indicate that 9.4% of children in the United States 2 to 17 years of age have ever had an ADHD diagnosis, including 2.4% of children 2 to 5 years of age (Danielson et al., 2018). In that national survey, 8.4% of children 2 to 17 years of age currently had ADHD, representing 5.4 million children (Danielson et al., 2018). Among children and adolescents with current ADHD, almost two-thirds were taking medication, and approximately half had received behavioral treatment of ADHD in the past year (Wolraich et al., 2019). Nearly one quarter had received neither type of treatment of ADHD (Danielson et al., 2018).

Children in some regions such as the southeast are diagnosed with ADHD more frequently than children in other parts of the country such as the northeast (e.g. North Carolina 12.8%, Connecticut 5.5%) (Visser et al., 2013). The lowest state-based rates of medicated ADHD were documented in 5 Western states (Nevada, California, Alaska, Hawaii, and New Mexico); the highest rates were documented in 5 Southern states (North Carolina, Louisiana, West Virginia, Arkansas, and Delaware) (Visser et al., 2013).

ADHD is more frequent in males than females in the general population, with a ratio of approximately to 2:1 in children and 1.6:1 in adults.

It is not clear whether the results from previous studies in European and Asian countries, where ADHD medication prevalence estimates are around 2% (Raman et al., 2018), will generalize to other settings, such as the United States, where the prevalence of diagnosed ADHD and ADHD medication use are higher (Raman et al., 2018; Xu et al., 2018). Countries like Hong Kong and Taiwan where Chinese culture is dominant, conservative attitudes and resistance toward ADHD medications are common (Man et al., 2017).

In 2016, 5.2% of all children 2 to 17 years of age in the United States were taking medication to treat ADHD (Danielson et al., 2018). Consistent with the observations that 80% of lifetime ADHD is diagnosed in the age range of

4–11 years, the peak increase in stimulant prescribing occurred between ages of 5 and 11 years (Kessler et al., 2007).

Rates of diagnosis and treatment of ADHD are higher among children born in August than among children born in September in states with a September 1 cutoff for kindergarten entry (Layton et al., 2018). Using data through 2015 from a large national insurance database, the authors found that in states with an age cutoff at September 1 for kindergarten entry, children born in August were significantly more likely to receive a diagnosis of ADHD than children born in September (Layton et al., 2018). Furthermore, children in these states who were born in August were more likely than children born in September to receive medical treatment for ADHD (Layton et al., 2018). These findings are consistent with the hypothesis that the context of behaviors within a grade or school class influences the likelihood of a diagnosis of ADHD (Layton et al., 2018).

What causes ADHD?

How ADHD develops in an individual or the pathogenesis of ADHD is not definitely known (Krull, 2022b). A genetic contribution to the pathogenesis of ADHD is supported by the increased risk of ADHD in first-degree relatives (e.g. parents, siblings and children) of patients with ADHD and twin studies from different countries that consistently provide heritability estimates of approximately 75% (Faraone et al., 2000; Levy et al., 1997; Thapar & Cooper, 2016; Thapar et al., 2013). In other words, genes contribute to 75% of ADHD and environment the rest 25% and this means we have little control in preventing this disorder from afflicting our children. Studying monozygotic twins, who share 100% same genes, provides us with a powerful tool to investigate the influence of experiences one twin has but not the other on various measures such as height, intelligence, etc.

Prenatal exposure to tobacco smoke is consistently associated with development of ADHD in case control and cohort studies (Huang et al., 2018; Sourander et al., 2019). Case-control and cohort studies are the types of observational studies done in the clinical research in order to find the association of exposure, with an outcome - and "cohort" means a group of people. It is uncertain whether this association is causal or mediated by unmeasured environmental or genetic confounders, which are the variables that are related to both exposure and outcomes and can cause spurious results (Gustavson et al., 2017; Schechter & Kollins, 2017; Thapar et al., 2009). This is another reason why people should stop smoking or never start smoking from the beginning.

Very low birth weight and the degree of prematurity convey a greater risk for ADHD; the more extreme the low birth weight, the greater the risk (Franz et al., 2018). Severe head injury can result in ADHD (Max et al., 1998) and ADHD is a risk factor for injury, including mild head injury (Chasle et al., 2016). Neurotoxin exposure (e.g., lead), infections (e.g., encephalitis), or alcohol exposure in utero have been correlated with subsequent ADHD (Donzelli et al., 2019; Dunn et al., 2019; Eichler et al., 2018; Yolton et al., 2014).

The effect of food additives (artificial colors and flavors, preservatives) on the behavior of children is an active area of investigation (Krull, 2022b). In March 2011, the Food Advisory Committee of the US Food and Drug Administration determined that existing data do not support a causal link between consumption of color additives and hyperactivity or other problematic behaviors in children (Food Advisory Committee of the US FDA). FDA regulates over 40 color additives used in food products, including nine synthetic dyes considered "certified color additives, which include FD&C Blue No. 1, FD&C Blue No. 2, FD&C Green No. 3, Orange B, Citrus Red No. 2, FD&C Red No. 3, FD&C Red No. 40, FD&C Yellow No. 5 and FD&C Yellow No. 6 (Food Advisory Committee of the US FDA).

A meta-analysis (an analysis of analyses) of 23 studies in which sugar was eliminated from the diet and/or children were challenged with sugar failed to support an association between sugar intake and hyperactivity, attention span, or cognitive functioning (Wolraich et al., 1995). However, a small effect of sugar on subsets of children could not be excluded (Krull, 2022b). A common-sense healthy diet is recommended not only for ADHD but also for the general well-being of the child and for the prevention of being overweight or obese. In patients failing to respond or with parents opposed to medication, omega-3 supplements may warrant a trial (Millichap & Yee, 2012).

The oligoallergenic diet (OAD) is an example of an elimination diet that may be used to assess the relationship between food sensitivity and behavior (Krull, 2022b). The OAD restricts intake to a few foods that are unlikely to cause allergy (e.g., turkey, lamb, rice, potato, banana, apple, pear, a few vegetables, water, salt and pepper) (Rojas & Chan, 2005). Based on the review of OAD trials in children with ADHD some children may have identifiable sensitivities to certain foods (Carter et al., 1993; Egger et al., 1985; Egger et al., 1992; Schmidt et al., 1997). Nonetheless food sensitivity plays no role in the majority of cases of ADHD (Krull, 2022b) and elimination diet can be disruptive to the household in general.

Neuropsychologic testing, which examines areas of memory, learning, attention, language and executive functioning suggests that patients with ADHD have impaired executive functions and/or difficulties with response inhibition (Barkley, 1999; Pennington & Ozonoff, 1996). What is an executive functioning? Executive functioning refers to the person's ability to organize his behaviors to perform a specific goal. Good executive functioning allows a person to identify problems, generate solutions, choose among them, follow through on the chosen strategy, and evaluate its effectiveness as the work progresses (Sadock et al., 2011). Differential response to reward and delay aversion also have been proposed as key deficits in ADHD (Sonuga-Barke et al., 2008). That is, children with ADHD either cannot tolerate a delay for an anticipated reward or are hyporesponsive to the reward, making their behavior difficult to shape by the normal reinforcements and punishments in the environment (Pliszka, 2022).

How do we diagnose ADHD in children and adolescents?

The clinician should perform a detailed interview with parents about each of the 18 ADHD symptoms listed in DSM-5 and if a symptom is present, inquire about its duration, severity, and frequency (Pliszka, 2022). After all the symptoms are assessed, the clinician should determine in which settings (school, work, home) impairment occurs (Pliszka, 2022). It is also important to gather data from the child school via teacher rating skills and /or review of schoolwork (Pliszka, 2022). The interview with a child or adolescent allows the clinician to identify signs or symptoms inconsistent with ADHD or suggestive of comorbid disorders (Pliszka, 2022). Careful assessment of mood, anxiety, and symptoms of thought disorder should be performed because parents may not be aware of such symptoms in their child (Pliszka, 2022). Moreover, medical professionals could play a key role by spending more time listening to children in order to get a deeper understanding of the individual nature of their problems, rather than relying on a more cursory approach that is limited to diagnosing and treating the symptoms of ADHD (Erler, 2013).

One of these diagnostic criteria of ADHD stipulates that several inattentive or hyperactive-impulsive symptoms were present prior to age 12 years and several inattentive or hyperactive-impulsive symptoms are present in 2 or more settings (for example at home, school or work; with friends or relatives; in other activities) (Amerian Psychiatric Association, 2013). Here we have a problem with specification. Longitudinal studies of individuals diagnosed with ADHD in childhood have noted that approximately

20% of participants are unable to accurately recall childhood symptoms (Mannuzza et al., 1993; Mannuzza et al., 2002). In addition, there is evidence to suggest that severity of childhood symptoms predicts more accurate recall (Kessler et al., 2005). Among studies specifically examining the accuracy of retrospective recall of ADHD symptoms (Henry, 1994; Mannuzza et al., 1998; Mannuzza et al., 2002), only one study used multiple reporters at follow-up to examine the accuracy of recall. These authors reported very low correlations across reporters for hyperactivity symptoms, but only slightly higher correlations for recall of other information such as body weight at a particular point in time.

It is important to distinguish between the behavioral symptoms of ADHD and the clinical syndrome of ADHD (Krull, 2022b). Inattentiveness, impulsivity, and hyperactivity occur to some extent in all children (Krull, 2022b). It is the persistence, pervasiveness, and functional complications of the behavioral symptoms that lead to a diagnosis of ADHD (Krull, 2022b). Clinicians need to try to obtain information from at least 2 teachers or other sources, such as coaches, school guidance counselors, or leaders of community activities in which the adolescent participates (Sibley et al., 2012).

This also means ADHD rarely occurs de novo in grown-ups and if the youngster is inattentive, impulsive or hyperactive only in one setting but does perfectly well in the other settings, more thorough investigation is needed to obtain further information in his home, academic or social environments to rule in or to rule out ADHD. Identifying reasons for any variability can provide valuable clinical insight into the adolescent's problems (Wolraich et al., 2019).

I have seen some adolescents, who report having difficulty focusing and staying on a task as they started high school and presenting with at least 6 symptoms in the inattentive type of ADHD. This is further supported by their parents, who state their children did very well academically in elementary and middle schools passing all the tests with flying colors but failing in high school. Based on DSM-5, they may not have ADHD since they do not meet the requirement of having several inattentive or hyperactive-impulsive symptoms prior to age 12 years. In this case we can think of another possibility: the existence of subthreshold childhood ADHD (Faraone & Biederman, 2016). In subthreshold cases, the onset of symptoms and impairment could be separated by many years, particularly among individuals with strong intellectual abilities and those living in supportive, well-structured childhood environments (Faraone & Biederman, 2016). Such intellectual and social scaffolding would help youth with ADHD to compensate in early life, only to decompensate into full ADHD syndrome when the scaffolding is removed (Faraone & Biederman, 2016).

So, let's talk about late-onset ADHD. What is late-onset ADHD? Findings from the Dunedin study (Moffitt et al., 2015) demonstrated that 90% of the individuals with adult ADHD at age 38 years had not met criteria for the disorder in childhood. Moffitt et al. (2015) make a hypothesis that there might be an adult-onset form of ADHD and that they found little evidence that neuropsychological dysfunction is the core etiologic feature of DSM-5 adult ADHD. In addition, Moffitt et al. (2015) suggest that there may be different etiologies for adult ADHD as childhood-ADHD-associated polygenic risk did not characterize adult ADHD. Agnew-Blais et al. (2016) suggests three possibilities in her article regarding late-onset ADHD. First, as mentioned above, individuals with late onset may have the same underlying liability for ADHD as those with childhood ADHD, but the disorder may be masked in childhood owing to protective factors, such as particularly supportive family environments or highly developed cognitive skills (Agnew-Blais et al., 2016). Second, individuals with late onset may not have ADHD at age 18 years but rather have another disorder with similar symptoms (Agnew-Blais et al., 2016). They found that those with late-onset ADHD exhibit elevated rates of anxiety, depression, and marijuana and alcohol dependence (Agnew-Blais et al., 2016). Third, late-onset adult ADHD could be a distinct disorder (Agnew-Blais et al., 2016). The late-onset ADHD group showed several characteristics that differ from childhood-onset ADHD, including a dissimilar sex composition (the late-onset group included more women) and lower heritability (Agnew-Blais et al., 2016). It is known that ADHD symptoms manifest in different ways throughout the patient's lifetime. As you can imagine, adults do not run about or climb in situations, where it is inappropriate. Instead, hyperactivity in adulthood is often experienced as a feeling of inner restlessness — an internal 'motor' that never stops — which makes it difficult for the individual to relax (Barkley et al., 2007). In adulthood, additional domains of impairment emerge and can include difficulties related to occupation, marriage and parenting (Faraone et al., 2015).

The pediatrician or other primary care clinician including child psychiatrist should initiate an evaluation for ADHD for any child or adolescent age 4 years to the 18th birthday who presents with academic or behavioral problems and symptoms of inattention, hyperactivity, or impulsivity (Wolraich et al., 2019). Note that there is insufficient evidence to recommend diagnosis or treatment for children younger than 4 years (other than parent training in behavior management [PTBM], which does not require a diagnosis to be applied); in instances in which ADHD-like symptoms in children younger than 4 years bring substantial impairment, the physician can consider making a referral for PTBM (Wolraich et al., 2019).

In the evaluation of a child or adolescent for ADHD, the physician should include a process to at least screen for comorbid conditions, including emotional or behavioral conditions (e.g. anxiety, depression, oppositional defiant disorder, conduct disorders, disruptive mood dysregulation disorder, bipolar disorder and substance use), developmental conditions (e.g. learning and language disorders, autism spectrum disorders), and physical conditions (e.g. tics, sleep apnea) (Wolraich et al., 2019).

Moreover, children with irritability and outbursts pose a serious therapeutic problem (Carlson & Klein, 2020). What mental health conditions may cause a youngster to be easily annoyed and made angry? A child with ADHD with emotion dysregulation usually has comorbid oppositional defiant disorder (ODD) and gets angry when he "doesn't get his way," but is otherwise relatively happy (Carlson & Klein, 2020). The child may go from "zero to sixty" but usually starts from "zero" (Carlson & Klein, 2020). This differs from a child with disruptive mood dysregulation disorder, who is always simmering just below the boiling point and therefore boils over more readily (Carlson & Klein, 2020).

According to DSM-5 (Amerian Psychiatric Association, 2013) oppositional defiant disorder (ODD) is defined as a pattern of angry/irritable mood, argumentative/defiant behavior, or vindictiveness lasting at least six months, and exhibited during interaction with at least one individual who is not a sibling. In addition, the disturbance in behavior is associated with distress in the individual or others in his immediate social context (e.g., family, peer group, work colleagues), or it impacts negatively on social, educational, occupational, or other important areas of functioning (Amerian Psychiatric Association, 2013). Based on DSM-5, the core feature of disruptive mood dysregulation disorder (DMDD) is chronic, persistently irritable or angry mood that is present between the severe temper outbursts (Amerian Psychiatric Association, 2013).

There is another group of children, who can present with severe irritability; mania or hypomania in bipolar I and II disorders, respectively. In children, as in adults, bipolar I disorder and bipolar II disorder manifest as an *episodic* illness with discrete episodes of mood perturbation (Amerian Psychiatric Association, 2013). In addition, during a manic episode, the change in mood must be accompanied by the onset, or worsening, of associated cognitive, behavioral, and physical symptoms (e.g., distractibility, increased goal-directed activity) (Amerian Psychiatric Association, 2013).

Irritability may also occur in, or serve as a forme fruste for, other conditions, the most relevant being depression and anxiety disorders (Carlson & Klein, 2020). This is supported by a number of lines of evidence, most notably follow-back studies of community samples that consistently report a connection between irritability and/or DMDD in childhood and anxiety and mood disorders in adults (Towbin et al., 2020).

Youth with ADHD frequently have low scores on standardized testing of academic achievement (Tannock, 2002). Academic impairment is commonly a result of the ADHD itself (Pliszka, 2022). Many months or years of not listening in class, not mastering material in an organized fashion, and not practicing academic skills (e.g., not doing homework) lead to an increasing gap between achievement and the patient's intellectual ability (Pliszka, 2022). If learning problems are secondary to ADHD, they should begin to improve within 2-3 months of successful treatment of the ADHD (although remedial tutoring may be needed) (Pliszka, 2022). In other cases, symptoms of comorbid learning and language disorders are present that cannot be accounted for by ADHD (Korrel et al., 2017; Pliszka, 2022). Specific learning disorder is defined by discrepancies in reading, mathematics, or written expression between the child's performance (ability to acquire and share information) and the child's intellectual capacity and age (Petti, 2022). When the child's performance consistently falls out of the acceptable range in one or more academic subjects, then the child becomes the focus of intense observation and documentation and is referred for evaluation to appropriate professionals (Grigorenko, 2007). An important qualifier here is that such observation, documentation, and evaluation are considered only for children whose performance is below that expected based on their general capacity to learn; thus, the concept of "unexpected' school failure is central to the definition of learning disorder (Grigorenko, 2007).

There is evidence that the diagnostic criteria for ADHD can be applied to preschool-aged children (Gadow et al., 2000; Harvey et al., 2009; Keenan & Wakschlag, 2000; Lahey et al., 1998; Pavuluri et al., 1999; Poblano & Romero, 2006; Sprafkin et al., 2002). A review of the literature, including the multisite study of the efficacy of methylphenidate in preschool-aged children, found that the DSM-5 criteria could appropriately identify children with ADHD (Evans et al., 2018).

The use of neuropsychological testing has not been found to improve diagnostic accuracy in most cases, although it may have benefit in clarifying the child or adolescent's learning strengths and weaknesses (Amerian Psychiatric Association, 2013).

4

What Other Mental Health Conditions Can Co-Occur With ADHD

The majority of both boys and girls with ADHD also meet diagnostic criteria for another mental disorder (Centers for Disease Control and Prevention (CDC), 2005; Elia et al., 2008). In the general population, oppositional defiant disorder (ODD) can occur at the same time with ADHD in approximately half of children with the combined presentation and about a quarter with the predominantly inattentive presentation (Amerian Psychiatric Association, 2013). The essential feature of oppositional defiant disorder is a frequent and persistent pattern of angry/irritable mood, argumentative/defiant behavior, or vindictiveness (Amerian Psychiatric Association, 2013). Risk factors for a diagnosis of ODD include lower socioeconomic status, harsh and inconsistent parenting practices, and family dysfunction (Drabick et al., 2011; Visser et al., 2013). Besides ODD, children with ADHD can also present with conduct disorder, which is characterized by a repetitive and persistent pattern of behavior in which the basic rights of others or major age-appropriate societal norms or rules are violated (Amerian Psychiatric Association, 2013). Risk factors for a diagnosis of conduct disorder (CD) are similar and include parental rejection and neglect, harsh discipline, physical or sexual abuse, frequent changes of caregivers, parent criminality, caregiver substance use, and neighborhood exposure to violence (Amerian Psychiatric Association, 2013). Boys are more likely to exhibit externalizing conditions like oppositional defiant disorder or conduct disorder (Cuffe et al., 2020; Elia et al., 2008; Gaub & Carlson, 1997). Recent research has established that girls with ADHD are more likely than boys to have a comorbid internalizing condition like anxiety or depression (Tung et al., 2016).

Youths with ADHD can also suffer from internalizing disorders such as anxiety or depression. If the full DSM-5 criteria for major depressive disorder are met in a child with ADHD, this most likely represents the full syndrome of MDD and not a state of demoralization due to ADHD symptoms (Biederman et al., 1998).

Comorbid ADHD and bipolar disorder involve greater complexity (Pliszka, 2022). In samples of youth selected for the presence of the *full syndrome* of a bipolar episode (mania, grandiosity, flight of ideas, or pressured speech), the rates of comorbidity with ADHD were as high as 90% in children (Geller, Warner, et al., 1998) and 68% in adolescents (Geller, Williams, et al., 1998).

Since children with ADHD frequently have overlapping symptoms of non-episodic irritability and dysregulated mood, this population and their treatment is an important area of exploration (Stringaris et al., 2010). Shaw et al. (2014) report a high rate (24%-50%) of emotional dysregulation in children with ADHD. DSM-5 created the category disruptive mood dysregulation disorder; one study showed that about one-fifth of children with ADHD ages 6 to 9 years met criteria for this disorder (Mulraney et al., 2016).

A variety of studies have shown that children with autism spectrum disorder have higher-than- expected prevalence of ADHD (range from 40% to 50%) and the children with ADHD show elevated rates of mild autistic symptoms, even in the absence of a formal autism spectrum disorder diagnosis (Visser et al., 2016).

Learning and language problems are common comorbid conditions with ADHD (Mueller & Tomblin, 2012).

What is the course and prognosis of ADHD?

ADHD is associated with reduced school performance and academic attainment, social rejection, and, in adults, poorer occupational performance, attainment, attendance, and higher probability of unemployment as well as elevated interpersonal conflict (Amerian Psychiatric Association, 2013). Meta-analytical results suggest that ADHD is associated with a 40-50% increase in the risk of injuries in children and adolescents (Lindemann et al., 2017; Ruiz-Goikoetxea et al., 2018). This study (Ghirardi et al., 2020) extends previous findings from studies conducted in Europe (Dalsgaard et al., 2015; Mikolajczyk et al., 2015; Raman et al., 2013) and Hong Kong (van den Ban et al., 2014) by showing that the injury risk reduction associated with concurrent ADHD medication use is consistent across sexes, age groups, injury type, and continents. Furthermore, although these studies did not differentiate between intentional and unintentional injury, they focused on unintentional injuries only, which represent a leading cause of disability and mortality in children and adolescents in the United States (Borse & Sleet, 2009).

Treating ADHD improved long-term outcomes but generally not to normal levels (Shaw et al., 2012). Treatment discontinuation also places individuals with ADHD at higher risk for catastrophic outcomes, such as motor vehicle crashes (Chang et al., 2014; Chang et al., 2017); criminality, including drug-related crimes (Lichtenstein et al., 2012) and violent reoffending (Chang, Lichtenstein, et al., 2016); depression (Chang, D'Onofrio, et al., 2016); interpersonal issues (Harstad & Levy, 2014); and other injuries (Dalsgaard et al., 2015; Raman et al., 2013).

Understanding the consequences of ADHD across childhood and adolescence has important implications for clinical practice, as many patients stop using their medication during adolescence (Zetterqvist et al., 2013).

In addition, some serious health issues in adulthood are elevated in those with ADHD, including obesity (Nigg et al., 2016) and hypertension (Fuemmeler et al., 2011).

Quality of life and attention-deficit/hyperactivity disorder
(Faraone et al., 2015)

How do we treat ADHD?

As in any psychiatric disorder, psychoeducation plays a vital role in the management of ADHD. Education includes information about the causes of ADHD, its associated morbidity, the potential for a compromise course, the rationale for treatments and plans for key life transitions (Nussey et al., 2013).

When children are diagnosed with ADHD, they are diagnosed with a condition that is supported with pharmacotherapy, behavioral interventions, and educational accommodations (Fadus et al., 2020). Before choosing a treatment, it is important to be aware of the child's psychosocial environment because treatments might be ineffective in 'chaotic' or potentially dangerous environments (Faraone et al., 2015).

To parents and care givers of children with ADHD we need to offer advice about the importance of positive parent-child contact, clear and appropriate rules about behavior and consistent management and structure in the child or young person's day (National Institute for Health and Care Excellence 2018).

While treatment often includes behavioral and educational strategies for associated problems, in children above 6 years, the core symptoms of ADHD are often treated with medications (Steingard et al., 2019). While nonstimulant options are available as monotherapy or combination treatment, stimulant medications have been and continue to be the most common first-line medication treatment for ADHD (Feldman et al., 2018; MTA Cooperative Group, 1999; Pediatrics. Subcomittee on ADHD, 2011). For most adolescents, stimulant medications are highly effective in reducing ADHD's core symptoms (Barbaresi et al., 2007).

Stimulant medications are slightly less effective and more poorly tolerated in preschoolers, compared to older children and adolescents (Greenhill et al., 2006). Preschool-aged children may experience increased mood lability and dysphoria with stimulant medications (Greenhill et al., 2006). A free list of the currently available, FDA-approved medications for ADHD is available online at www. ADHDMedicationGuide.com (Wolraich et al., 2019).

Nevertheless, before initiating therapy with stimulant medications, it is important to obtain the child or adolescent's history of specific cardiac symptoms in addition to the family history of sudden death, cardiovascular symptoms, Wolff-Parkinson-White syndrome, hypertrophic cardiomyopathy, and long QT syndrome (Wolraich et al., 2019).

Parents and patients should be cautioned that medications primarily target symptoms and do not alter underlying mechanisms or immediately impart social-behavioral skills or address problematic learned behaviors, including negative attributions, demoralization, and low self-esteem (Steingard et al., 2022). The conflation of these associated problems with the core symptoms when attempting to assess treatment response can lead to the misperception of a failed medication trial (Steingard et al., 2022).

Methylphenidate (MPH) and amphetamine (AMP) are the core stimulants that are used to treat ADHD (Steingard et al., 2019). The primary action of stimulants is to increase the synaptic availability of dopamine and norepinephrine, although AMP) and MPH achieve this in slightly different ways (Steingard et al., 2019). In a recent meta-analysis of comparative efficacy and tolerability, Cortese et al. (2018) have suggested that MPH may be the preferred agent in children and adolescents, while AMP may be preferred in adults. A recent meta-analysis suggests that different types of stimulants can either increase or decrease irritability in youth with ADHD (Stuckelman et al., 2017).

The typical response duration or behavioral half-life for immediate-release formulations is 3–5 hours (Steingard et al., 2019). Thus, until the advent of longer acting formulations of stimulant medication, treatment required the administration of multiple doses throughout the day (Steingard et al., 2019). This created encumbrances that often interfered with access to effective treatment (Steingard et al., 2019). Immediate-release formulations continue to play a role in the overall management of ADHD (Steingard et al., 2019). They can be useful in the initial treatment of young children, those with autism spectrum disorder or intellectual disability, and managing afternoon or evening functioning (Steingard et al., 2019). However, the extended-release formulations have become the core of treatment and there is no need to initiate treatment with immediate-release and then transition to extended-release formulations (Steingard et al., 2019).

There has been a marked increase in the number of available stimulant formulations with the emphasis on long-acting formulations, and the introduction of several novel delivery systems such as orally dissolving tablets (ODT), chewable tablets, extended-release liquid formulations, transdermal patches, and novel ''beaded'' technology (Steingard et al., 2019). Extended-release formulations loosely fall in to the range of medium duration (6–10 hours), long duration (8–12 hours), and very long duration (>12 hours) and a number of the formulations can accommodate patients who have difficulty swallowing oral dosage forms (Steingard et al., 2019). Treatment with an extended-release formulation can be supplemented or ''sculpted'' with an additional dose of immediate-release medication to provide an enhanced response with the morning dose or to extend coverage into the early evening if required (Steingard et al., 2019). Dosing is typically started at the lowest available dosage strength and titrated against response and tolerability to determine the optimal dose (Steingard et al., 2019). In addition to these new formulations, our knowledge of individual variability with regard to response and metabolism has also advanced and contributes to a more nuanced approach to treatment (Steingard et al., 2019). This widened armamentarium hopefully will lead to greater personalizing of ADHD treatment in hopes of improving adherence and long-term outcomes (Steingard et al., 2019).

The mean elimination half-life is reported as ranging from 9 to 11 hours for d-AMP and 11 to 14 hours for l-AMP (Steingard et al., 2019). Furthermore, when combined in a racemic mixture, the two isomers compete metabolically and thus prolong the elimination of both isomers, possibly extending the duration of response (Markowitz & Patrick, 2017).

These compounds appear to have comparable clinical efficacy, yet there are individuals who responded preferentially to only one compound (Coghill et al., 2014; Stein et al., 2011). Acute response rate to stimulant treatment is 70%, but the response rate can increase to close to 90%

with carefully managed sequential trials of different stimulants and stimulant formulations that are carefully titrated (Coghill et al., 2014; Stein et al., 2011). Stimulant medications can be effectively titrated on a 7-day basis, but in urgent situations, they may be effectively titrated in as few as 3 days (Jensen et al., 2001).

As treatment progresses, if the treatment effect is "lost" over time, the clinician must first assess whether the changes are a reflection of loss of medication effect on core symptoms or something else, such as environmental factors (e.g. a behavioral response to new stressors), developmental or maturation factors, the emergence of a previously subthreshold comorbid disorder, or nonadherence (Steingard et al., 2022).

When the child does not respond to stimulants or cannot tolerate these due to side effects or adverse reactions, non-stimulant medications deserve a trial. One of those medications is called Atomoxetine, also known as Strattera. Atomoxetine is a compound that was originally developed, but not marketed, as an antidepressant (Steingard et al., 2022). After a program of clinical trials, atomoxetine was approved by the FDA in 2002 for use in treating ADHD in children and adults (Michelson et al., 2001; Spencer et al., 2001; Spencer et al., 1998). Although some response to atomoxetine can be observed within the first week of administration, further gradual improvement typically occurs over the ensuing 4-6 weeks (Steingard et al., 2022). Atomoxetine produces a more sustained response than to the stimulants and can be given once a day, either in the morning or in the evening (Michelson et al., 2002; Newcorn et al., 2009). A series of randomized control trials (RCTs) established that atomoxetine was effective in treating ADHD in children, adolescents, and adults (Hammerness et al., 2009; Simpson & Plosker, 2004). However, atomoxetine is considered to be a second-tier agent, after the stimulants (Steingard et al., 2022). When compared with placebo common side effects that occur more frequently with atomoxetine include decreased appetite, somnolence, abdominal discomfort, nausea, vomiting, fatigue, and dry mouth (Steingard et al., 2022). Similar to methylphenidate (Ritalin), atomoxetine is associated with mild increases in heart rate and blood pressure and initial weight loss (Steingard et al., 2022). Moreover, atomoxetine can lead to treatment-emergent increases in agitation, irritability, and anxiety (Steingard et al., 2022). Gradual introduction of the drug at lower doses might mitigate this effect (Steingard et al., 2022). Although the combination of atomoxetine and a stimulant does not have an FDA-approved indication, it is used widely in clinical practice (Steingard et al., 2022).

α2-Adrenergic receptor agonists (α2 agonists) were originally approved as centrally acting antihypertensive agents (Steingard et al., 2022). Two compounds in this class, clonidine and guanfacine, have been systematically studied in the treatment of ADHD in children and adolescents, strengthening our understanding of the role of noradrenergic mechanisms and this class of drugs in the treatment of ADHD (Arnsten et al., 1988; Arnsten et al., 2007; Arnsten et al., 1996; Biederman & Spencer, 1999). Guanfacine ER (Intuniv) was approved by the FDA for use in the treatment of ADHD in 2009 (Steingard et al., 2022). Clonidine ER (Kapvay) was approved by the FDA in 2010 for use in the treatment of ADHD in 6- to 17-year-olds (Steingard et al.,

2022). Both drugs were approved as monotherapy or in combination with a stimulant (Steingard et al., 2022) Meta-analyses have suggested that the overall effect size of the α2 agonists is lower than that of the stimulant medications and the α2 agonists are more likely to be associated with treatment discontinuation secondary to adverse effects (Hirota et al., 2014).

α2-Adrenergic receptor agonists are FDA approved in combination with a stimulant (Steingard et al., 2022). The rationale for combining these agents with stimulants includes the following suppositions: 1) combined treatment may be superior for achieving desired behavioral outcome, 2) combined treatment may be superior for achieving desired cognitive improvement, 3) synergy between these compounds may allow for lower doses of each compound that will reduce adverse events, and 4) the sedative effects of the α2 agents may provide an alternative late afternoon or early evening treatment strategy (Steingard et al., 2022). It appears that adding an α2 agent to a stimulant can modestly improve the behavioral response achieved with stimulant monotherapy but can lead to increased rates of somnolence, sedation, and fatigue (Steingard et al., 2022). There is no clear positive effect on cognitive function (Hirota et al., 2014).

Viloxazine hydrochloride is a norepinephrine reuptake inhibitor with selective serotonin modulation activity that has been used in Europe as an antidepressant for many years; results of a phase III study have been published (Nasser et al., 2020). Statistically significant improvements in ADHD-Rating Scale-5 total score was observed in both the 100- or

200-mg/day treatment groups compared with placebo at week 1 and through week 6 (Nasser et al., 2020).

Bupropion, an antidepressant as well as a medication used for smoking cessation, is one of the non-stimulatory medications, that can be employed as a treatment option for children with ADHD. Although its efficacy is generally known to be lower than stimulants, it remains a viable option if a child cannot tolerate stimulant medications or are not eligible for stimulants. Strict dosing guidelines should be adhered to in order to minimize the risk of seizures as it can lower seizure threshold.

Modafinil was originally released in France in 1984 and then approved in the United States in 1998 as a "vigilance-enhancing' agent for the treatment of narcolepsy (Minzenberg & Carter, 2008). Although the mechanism of action remains elusive, some studies suggest that modafinil may potentiate both dopamine and norepinephrine neurotransmission (Minzenberg & Carter, 2008) as methylphenidate and amphetamine stimulants act. Modafinil has not been approved by the FDA for use in ADHD, and its use in clinical practice is limited because of concern regarding the potential for serious allergic reactions, including but not limited to, Stevens-Johnson syndrome (Steingard et al., 2022).

From a clinical perspective, the increasing evidence that ADHD medication seems to be associated with a reduction of severe outcomes, including injuries, but also criminality (Lichtenstein et al., 2012), substance use disorder (Quinn et al., 2017), and transport accidents (Chang et al., 2014; Chang et al., 2017), may be an additional factor to consider when weighing benefits against risks of ADHD medications.

Clinicians should partner with families to determine whether the possible changes in adult height (1.5 inches shorter) and weight and BMI (greater risks of obesity) may be outweighed by the risks of not treating the child's ADHD (Greenhill et al., 2020). Nevertheless, adherence to stimulants is modest, especially in adolescents who often discontinue medication, despite persistence of symptoms and impairments (Adler & Nierenberg, 2010). The UK National Institute for Health and Care Excellence (2018) recommends to encourage parents and caregivers to oversee ADHD medication for children and adolescents.

At the same time, especially with adolescents and young adults, a periodic reassessment to find out whether it is time to try to discontinue medication treatment needs to be made as their hyperactivity symptoms tend to dissipate over the course of time.

Some reports have documented the efficacy of stimulants (Connor et al., 2002), extended-release guanfacine (Connor et al., 2010) and atomoxetine for the treatment of co-morbid oppositional defiant disorder symptoms (Newcorn et al., 2005).

Although some academic performance problems associated with symptoms of ADHD (for example, homework completion) can improve with treatment, medication cannot replace missing skills, improve academic achievement scores or ameliorate specific learning disabilities (Langberg et al., 2011).

The available scientific literature does not provide sufficient evidence to support the clinical utility of pharmacogenetics given that the genetic variants assayed by these tools have generally not been fully studied with respect to medication effects on ADHD-related symptoms and/or impairment, study findings are inconsistent, or effect sizes are not of sufficient size to ensure clinical utility (Brown & Bishop, 2015; Bruxel et al., 2014; Froehlich et al., 2010; Joensen et al., 2017; Kambeitz et al., 2014; Kieling et al., 2010). For that reason, these pharmacogenetics tools are not recommended (Wolraich et al., 2019).

Some psychosocial treatments for children and adolescents with ADHD have been demonstrated to be effective for the treatment of ADHD, including behavioral therapy and training interventions (Evans et al., 2018; Pelham & Fabiano, 2008; Pelham et al., 1998; Sonuga-Barke et al., 2001). The combination of medication management and behavioral therapy allowed for the use of lower stimulant dosages, possibly reducing the risk of adverse effects.

Behavioral interventions include modifications in the physical and social environment that are designed to change behavior using rewards and nonpunitive consequences (Charach et al., 2013; Krull, 2022a; Wolraich et al., 2019). Behavioral techniques that are used for children with ADHD include positive reinforcement, time-out, response cost (withdrawing rewards or privileges when unwanted or problem behavior occurs), and token economy (a combination of positive reinforcement and response cost) (Floet et al., 2010; Krull, 2022b).

Behavioral interventions are preferred to medication as the initial intervention for preschool children with ADHD and are adjuncts to medication for school-aged children and adolescents (Carlson et al., 1992; Dulcan, 1997; Kolko et al., 1999; National Institute for Health and Care Excellence 2018; Wolraich et al., 2019). Behavioral interventions also can be used for children who have problems with inattention, hyperactivity or impulsivity but do not meet criteria for ADHD (Wolraich et al., 2019).

Parent-child behavioral therapy is aimed at improving parent-child relationships through enhanced parenting techniques (Kaplan & Adesman, 2011). Behavior interventions are most effective if parents understand the principles of behavioral therapy (ie, identification of antecedents and altering the consequences of behavior) and the techniques are consistently implemented (Floet et al., 2010; Kaplan & Adesman, 2011).

Behavior therapy and environmental changes that can be used by parents or teachers to shape the behavior of children with ADHD include (American Academy of Pediatrics 2001):

- Managing a daily schedule
- Keeping distractions to a minimum
- Providing specific and logical places for the child to keep his or her schoolwork, toys, and clothes
- Setting small, reachable goals
- Rewarding positive behavior (e.g., with a "token economy")
- Identifying unintentional reinforcement of negative behaviors

- Using charts and checklists to help the child stay "on task"
- Limiting choices
- Finding activities in which the child can be successful (e.g., hobbies, sports)
- Using calm discipline (e.g., time out, distraction, removing the child from the situation)

There are essentially 2 categories of school-based services for students with ADHD (Wolraich et al., 2019). The first category includes interventions that are intended to help the student independently meet age-appropriate academic and behavioral expectations (Wolraich et al., 2019). Examples of these interventions include daily report cards, training interventions, point systems, and academic remediation of skills (Wolraich et al., 2019). If successful, the student's impairment will resolve, and the student will no longer need services (Wolraich et al., 2019). The second category is intended to provide changes in the student's program so his or her ADHD-related problems no longer result in failure and cause distress to parents, teachers, and the student (Harrison et al., 2013). These services are referred to as "accommodations" and include extended time to complete tests and assignments, reduced homework demands, the ability to keep study materials in class, and provision of the teacher's notes to the student (Wolraich et al., 2019). These services are intended to allow the student to accomplish his work successfully and communicate that the student's impairment is acceptable (Wolraich et al., 2019). Accommodations make the student's impairment acceptable and are separate from interventions aimed at improving the students' skills or behaviors (Wolraich et al., 2019). In the absence of such interventions, long- term accommodations may lead to reduced expectations and can lead to the need for accommodations to be maintained throughout the student's education (Wolraich et al., 2019).

Overall, behavioral family approaches may be helpful to some adolescents and their families, and school-based training interventions are well established (Evans et al., 2018; Sibley et al., 2016). Transition to adult care is an important component of the chronic care model for ADHD (Wolraich et al., 2019). Planning for the transition to adult care is an ongoing process that may culminate after high school or, perhaps, after college (Wolraich et al., 2019). To foster a smooth transition, it is best to introduce components at the start of high school, at about14 years of age, and specifically focus during the 2 years preceding high school completion (Wolraich et al., 2019).

What are the side effects of stimulants including Adderall?

Stimulants' most common short-term adverse effects are appetite loss, abdominal pain, headaches, and sleep disturbance such as delays in sleep onset (Steingard et al., 2019; Wolraich et al., 2019). These adverse effects are often transitory, and adjustments in dosage, timing, or changing formulations can be helpful, as well as consultation regarding meal management, especially with younger children, and sleep hygiene (Steingard et al., 2019). The management of appetite reduction includes monitoring appetite, weight, height and body mass index (BMI) every 6 months and differentiating between pretreatment eating problems and medication-induced eating problems (Cortese et al., 2013). If weight loss is a clinical concern, the following strategies are recommended by the UK National Institute for Health and Care Excellence (2018): taking medication either with or after food, rather than before meals, taking additional meals or snacks early in the morning or late in the evening when stimulant effects have worn off, obtaining dietary advice, consuming high-calorie foods of good nutritional value such as avocado, walnuts, Greek yogurt, salmon, peanut butter, eggs, whole milk, sweet potatoes and almonds, taking a planned break from treatment and changing medication. An uncommon significant adverse effect of stimulants is the occurrence of hallucinations and other psychotic symptoms (Mosholder et al., 2009). Hallucinations are a very rare side effect that typically remit with discontinuation (Coghill et al., 2014).

Reported cumulative exposure to stimulant medication in methylphenidate equivalents (ME) have steady increased over decades, as shown in follow-up studies of ADHD on long-term medication in the 1960s with an average exposure of 34,350 mg (Kramer et al., 2000), in the 1970s with an average exposure of 36,710 mg (Satterfield et al., 1979), in the 1980s with an average exposure of 42,268 mg (Harstad et al., 2014), all showing no association between dose and duration of stimulants and adult height (Swanson et al., 2017).

However, the more recent study found that 16 years of consistent treatment with stimulants of children with ADHD in the MTA was associated with a reduction in adult height, and an increase in weight and body mass index (Greenhill et al., 2020). Other paired comparisons suggested that ADHD subgroups in adulthood were heavier and had higher BMI than the LNCG (local normative comparison group), consistent with reports of an association of youth with ADHD and adult obesity (Cortese et al., 2016; Fliers et al., 2013; Hanć & Cortese, 2018).

How Adderall became available on the market?

Although racemic α-methylphenethylamine (amphetamine) was discovered by Barger and Dale in 1910, it was not until 1927 that this molecule was first synthesized by the chemist, G. A. Alles, whilst he was searching for a less costly and more easily synthesized substitute for ephedrine (Heal et al., 2013). The trade name 'Benzedrine®' for racemic α-methyl-phenethylamine was registered by the pharmaceutical company, Smith, Kline and French (Heal et al., 2013). 'Amphetamine', which is the generic name for Benzedrine devised by the Council on Pharmacy and Chemistry of the American Medical Association, was not adopted until many years later (Heal et al., 2013). Smith, Kline and French introduced Benzedrine onto the market in 1935 as a treatment for narcolepsy (for which it is still used today), mild depression, post-encephalitic Parkinsonism and a raft of other disorders (Bett, 1946; Guttmann & Sargant, 1937; Tidy, 1938). In 1937, Smith, Kline and French commenced marketing of d-amphetamine under the trade name of Dexedrine® (Heal et al., 2013). Sales of Benzedrine and Dexedrine in chemist stores were unrestricted until 1939, when these drugs could only be obtained either on prescription from a registered medical practitioner or by signing the Poison Register (Bett, 1946). It was Bradley

(1937) who first reported the beneficial effects of Benzedrine in treating children with severe behavioral problems, who would now be diagnosed as suffering from attention deficit/hyperactivity disorder (ADHD) (Amerian Psychiatric Association, 2013). Currently, the only use of *l*-amphetamine in ADHD medications is in mixed salts/mixed enantiomers amphetamine (MES-amphetamine), which consists of a 3:1 enantiomeric mixture *d*-amphetamine: *l*-amphetamine salts that is available in both immediate-release (Adderall®, generic) and extended-release (Adderall XR®, generic) formulations (Heal et al., 2013).

Why stimulants including Adderall are overprescribed and what are the current concerns?

Parents think that stimulants will solve all the problems their children face as if they will increase the cognitive abilities and reasoning skills of their children. The stimulants per se will not improve their grades in school or improve their work performance automatically. The medications will provide them with only enhanced capability to focus. They are like glasses to people with eyesight problems. They still need to invest their time and energy into their work or study to succeed. It may reflect the trend set by the first antidepressant, Fluoxetine (Prozac). It imparted us the notion of "controllability" of our moods by means of medication. We can be happy or happier by swallowing a simple pill. By the same token we can be efficient or more efficient by using a stimulant. Our brains will work more effectively with sharp and focused attention. If we can maneuver whatever and however we can, why we don't use it for improvement of our emotions, behavior and even intelligence. Admittedly these psychostimulants can be life changing for a certain sector of latency stage boys and girls and their families in the US and globally. However, at the same time the potential overdiagnosis of ADHD and overuse of stimulants in pediatric population needs to be guarded in the context of massive advertisements by big pharmaceutical companies and high expectations of parents for their children. I think a small portion of the parents want their children to be happy and successful in their education and future career by taking advantage of accommodations, i.e. get an additional one-half hour for examinations and tests and to have an upper hand in being accepted in prestigious Ivy schools in the US. However, the use of stimulants in their youth may place them vulnerable to potential substance use disorder and eating disorders by increasing addiction potential and suppressing appetite, respectively.

Note that, unless they previously received a diagnosis, to meet DSM-5 criteria for ADHD, adolescents must have some reported or documented manifestations of inattention or hyperactivity/impulsivity before age 12. Therefore, clinicians must establish that an adolescent had manifestations of ADHD before age 12 and strongly consider whether a mimicking or comorbid condition, such as substance use, depression, and/or anxiety, is present (Sibley et al., 2012). Adolescent patients may also attempt to obtain stimulant medication to enhance performance (i.e., academic, athletic, etc.) by feigning symptoms (Harrison et al., 2007).

In addition, diversion of ADHD medication (i.e., its use for something other than its intended medical purposes) is a special concern among adolescents. Clinicians should monitor the adolescent's symptoms and prescription refill requests for signs of misuse or diversion of ADHD medication, including by parents, classmates, or other acquaintances of the adolescent (Wolraich et al., 2019). As a result, child and adolescent psychiatrists should counsel their patients and families on the importance of securing prescription medication safely, not sharing with friends or family, and disposing of unused medication (Thurstone, 2019). Many pharmacies have disposal kiosks for un- used medication (Thurstone, 2019). The Food and Drug Administration (FDA) recommends against flushing medications down the toilet (Thurstone, 2019). Instead, most drugs can be safely disposed of in the trash. Before throwing in the trash, the FDA makes 3 recommendations. First, patients should remove drugs from containers and mix with something undesirable such as cat litter. Second, patients should seal the medication in a container or bag to avoid spillage. Third, patients should scratch out their personal information from the pill bottle. Medications that should not be thrown in the trash are fentanyl patches and metered-dose inhalers.

Non-medical use of prescription stimulants is a growing public health concern, particularly among college students, of whom nearly one-fifth use prescription stimulants non-medically (Benson et al., 2015). College students report a variety of motivations for using prescription stimulants non-medically including cognitive enhancement, to get high or prolong the effects of other substances, and weight loss

(Benson et al., 2015). Unhealthy weight management practices commonly endorsed among individuals reporting non-medical use of prescription stimulants for weight-related purposes primarily include binge eating and purging, especially objective binge eating (Gibbs et al., 2016), vomiting for weight loss (Gibbs et al., 2016; Jeffers & Benotsch, 2014; Striley et al., 2017) and use of laxatives, diet pills or diuretics (Gibbs et al., 2016; Jeffers et al., 2013; Jeffers & Benotsch, 2014; Striley et al., 2017). Disordered eating was a significant predictor of non-medical, but not medical use of prescription stimulants among college students (Nutley et al., 2020).

Neuroethical Issues

Drugs that improve facets of cognition such as attention, learning, memory and executive functions are known as pharmacological cognitive enhancers (PCEs) (Morein-Zamir, 2008; Sahakian et al., 2010). These drugs alter neurotransmitter modulation of cognition leading to improvements in cognitive deficits in patients with traumatic brain injury (TBI) (Teitelman, 2001), depression (Vaishnavi et al., 2006), addiction (Shearer et al., 2009), multiple sclerosis (Kraft & Bowen, 2005; Nieves & Lang, 2002; Zifko et al., 2002), Parkinson's disease, and those suffering from Alzheimer's disease (AD), schizophrenia, and attention-deficit/hyperactivity disorder (ADHD) (Mohamed & Sahakian, 2012). Neurotransmitters are chemicals that relay messages between neurons in the brain or neurons and muscles in the limbs and other parts of the body. Serotonin, norepinephrine and dopamine are some of the important neurotransmitters in the field of psychiatry. Pharmacological cognitive enhancers (PCEs) can effectively improve core symptoms, abnormal behaviors, self-esteem, cognition, social and family function in ADHD patients (Sahakian & Morein-Zamir, 2007). Methylphenidate has been shown to enhance spatial working memory performance in healthy adults (Elliott et al., 1997). The spatial working memory test is a self-ordered search task which requires subjects to search through a spatial array of colored boxes for "tokens" (Elliott et al., 1997; Owen et al., 1990).

Based on the findings from qualitative research with non-medical users, Vrecko (2013) reports that stimulants' effects on users' emotions and feelings are important contributor to users' perceptions of improved academic performance

Nevertheless, the increase in lifestyle use of pharmacological cognitive enhancers (PCEs) by healthy people raises numerous ethical issues that inform the growing field of neuroethics (Mohamed & Sahakian, 2012). Neuroethics is the study of the ethical, legal and social questions that arise when scientific findings about the brain are carried into medical practice, legal interpretations and health and social policy (Marcus, 2002). There is a concern that pharmacological cognitive enhancers (PCEs) will threaten our notion of personhood and will dampen essential characteristics of what it means to be human (Farah et al., 2004; President's Council on Bioethics 2003). As a consequence, enhancing the brain and higher cognitive processes demands strong ethical considerations and a practical policy framework (Mohamed & Sahakian, 2012).

The issues of using pharmacologic cognitive enhancers include the potential harms and long- term side effects that they might have in healthy people, particularly in adolescents where the brain is still in development (Mohamed & Sahakian, 2012). A recent study showed that modafinil blocked dopamine transporters and increased dopamine in the caudate, putamen and nucleus accumbens in healthy human brain (Volkow et al., 2009), which are areas in a network known to be involved in drug-seeking behavior and addiction (Volkow & Li, 2004). To date, there have been no randomized psychopharmacological trials investigating the long-term effects of pharmacological cognitive enhancer (PCE) drugs on healthy people.

With regard to personal autonomy, there are ethical concerns about healthy people being coerced or even forced into using a pharmacological cognitive enhancer (PCE) (Mohamed & Sahakian, 2012). For example, authorities in the USA ordered a mentally ill inmate in criminal proceedings to take psychotropic medication to improve his competence to stand trial and be executed (Boire & Ruiz-Sierra, 2003; Randall, 2004). There is also a considerable potential for indirect coercion resulting from a highly demanding 24/7 society where people feel compelled to take pharmaco-logical cognitive enhancers (PCE) to meet social or workplace demands (Mohamed & Sahakian, 2012). However, the use of PCEs to enhance cognition is one solution to improving the individual and society (Mohamed & Sahakian, 2012). Indeed, there are other methods of boosting cognition, including education and exercise (Sahakian & Morein-Zamir, 2011). For instance, physical exercise can improve learning and memory (Creer et al., 2010; Hillman et al., 2008). Physical activity, and aerobic fitness training in particular, can have a positive effect on multiple aspects of brain function and cognition (Hillman et al., 2008). Physical activity can have beneficial effects throughout the lifespan, even for individuals with neurodegenerative diseases (Cotman et al., 2007; Heyn et al., 2004). Another argument against their use is that they might further exacerbate the ever-growing disparity and inequality in society, especially if only the wealthy can access them (Mohamed & Sahakian, 2012). On the flip side of the coin, enhancing cognition might lead to dramatic social benefits by reducing natural inequality and promoting social justice (Savulescu, 2006). For instance, a 3% population-wide increase in IQ would reduce poverty rates by 25% (Weiss, 1998) and would lead to an annual economic gain of US$165-$195 billion and up to 1.5% GDP growth (Salkever, 1995; Schwartz, 1994). Mohamed and Sahakian (2012) recommend that neuropsychopharmacologists need to work together with social scientists, philosophers, ethicists, policy makers, and teachers to actively discuss the ethical consequences of pharmacological cognitive enhancer (PCE) usage.

References:

1. Adler, L. D., & Nierenberg, A. A. (2010). Review of medication adherence in children and adults with ADHD. Postgrad Med, 122(1), 184-191. https://doi.org/10.3810/pgm.2010.01.2112

2. Agnew-Blais, J. C., Polanczyk, G. V., Danese, A., Wertz, J., Moffitt, T. E., & Arseneault, L. (2016). Evaluation of the Persistence, Remission, and Emergence of Attention-Deficit/Hyperactivity Disorder in Young Adulthood. JAMA Psychiatry, 73(7), 713-720. https://doi.org/10.1001/jamapsychiatry.2016.0465

3. Amerian Psychiatric Association. (2013). Diagnostic and statistical manual of mental disorders : DSM-5 (5th ed.). American Psychiatric Association.

4. Amerian Psychiatric Association. (c1970). Diagnostic and statistical manual of mental disorders, Second Edition (DSM II) (2nd ed.). American Psychiatric Association.

5. Amerian Psychiatric Association. (c1980). Diagnostic and statistical manual of mental disorders, Third Edition (DSM III) (3rd ed.). American Psychiatric Association.

6. Amerian Psychiatric Association. (c1987). Diagnostic and statistical manual of mental disorders, Third Edition-Revised (DSM III R) (3rd-Revised ed.). American Psychiatric Association.

7. American Academy of Pediatrics (2001). Understanding ADHD. Information for parents about attention-deficit/hyperactivity disorder. American Academy of Pediatrics.

8. Arnsten, A. F., Cai, J. X., & Goldman-Rakic, P. S. (1988). The alpha-2 adrenergic agonist guanfacine improves memory in aged monkeys without sedative or hypotensive side effects: evidence for alpha-2 receptor subtypes. J

Neurosci, 8(11), 4287-4298.
https://doi.org/10.1523/jneurosci.08-11-04287.1988

9. Arnsten, A. F., Scahill, L., & Findling, R. L. (2007). alpha2-Adrenergic receptor agonists for the treatment of attention-deficit/hyperactivity disorder: emerging concepts from new data. J Child Adolesc Psychopharmacol, 17(4), 393-406. https://doi.org/10.1089/cap.2006.0098

10. Arnsten, A. F., Steere, J. C., & Hunt, R. D. (1996). The contribution of alpha 2-noradrenergic mechanisms of prefrontal cortical cognitive function. Potential significance for attention-deficit hyperactivity disorder. Arch Gen Psychiatry, 53(5), 448-455. https://doi.org/10.1001/archpsyc.1996.01830050084013

11. Barbaresi, W. J., Katusic, S. K., Colligan, R. C., Weaver, A. L., & Jacobsen, S. J. (2007). Modifiers of long-term school outcomes for children with attention-deficit/hyperactivity disorder: does treatment with stimulant medication make a difference? Results from a population-based study. J Dev Behav Pediatr, 28(4), 274-287. https://doi.org/10.1097/DBP.0b013e3180cabc28

12. Barkley, R. A. (1999). Theories of attention-deficit/hyperactivity disorder. In H. C. Quay, Hogan, A.E. (Ed.), Handbook of Disruptive Behavior Disorders. Kluwer Academic/Plenium.

13. Barkley, R. A., Murphy, K. R., & Fischer, M. (2007). ADHD in Adults: What the Sicence Says. Guildford.

14. Barkley, R. A., & Peters, H. (2012). The earliest reference to ADHD in the medical literature? Melchior Adam Weikard's description in 1775 of "attention deficit" (Mangel der Aufmerksamkeit, Attentio Volubilis). J Atten Disord, 16(8), 623-630. https://doi.org/10.1177/1087054711432309

15. Benson, K., Flory, K., Humphreys, K. L., & Lee, S. S. (2015). Misuse of stimulant medication among college students: a comprehensive review and meta-analysis. Clin Child Fam Psychol Rev, 18(1), 50-76. https://doi.org/10.1007/s10567-014-0177-z

16. Bett, W. R. (1946). Benzedrine sulphate in clinical medicine; a survey of the literature. Postgrad Med J, 22(250), 205-218. https://doi.org/10.1136/pgmj.22.250.205

17. Biederman, J., Mick, E., & Faraone, S. V. (1998). Depression in attention deficit hyperactivity disorder (ADHD) children: "true" depression or demoralization? J Affect Disord, 47(1-3), 113-122. https://doi.org/10.1016/s0165-0327(97)00127-4

18. Biederman, J., Mick, E., & Faraone, S. V. (2000). Age-dependent decline of symptoms of attention deficit hyperactivity disorder: impact of remission definition and symptom type. Am J Psychiatry, 157(5), 816-818. https://doi.org/10.1176/appi.ajp.157.5.816

19. Biederman, J., & Spencer, T. (1999). Attention-deficit/hyperactivity disorder (ADHD) as a noradrenergic disorder. Biol Psychiatry, 46(9), 1234-1242. https://doi.org/10.1016/s0006-3223(99)00192-4

20. Boire, R. G., & Ruiz-Sierra, J. (2003). Supreme court upholds right to refuse mind-altering drugs. http://www.cognitiveliberty.org/news/US_v_Sell_decision.htm

21. Borse, N., & Sleet, D. A. (2009). CDC Childhood Injury Report: Patterns of Unintentional Injuries Among 0- to 19-Year Olds in the United States, 2000-2006. Fam Community Health, 32(2), 189. https://doi.org/10.1097/01.Fch.0000347986.44810.59

22. Bradley, C. (1937). Behaviour of children receiving Benzedrine. Am J Psychiatry, 94, 577-585.

23. Brown, J. T., & Bishop, J. R. (2015). Atomoxetine pharmacogenetics: associations with pharmacokinetics, treatment response and tolerability. Pharmacogenomics, 16(13), 1513-1520. https://doi.org/10.2217/pgs.15.93

24. Bruxel, E. M., Akutagava-Martins, G. C., Salatino-Oliveira, A., Contini, V., Kieling, C., Hutz, M. H., & Rohde, L. A. (2014). ADHD pharmacogenetics across the life cycle: New findings and perspectives. Am J Med Genet B Neuropsychiatr Genet, 165b(4), 263-282. https://doi.org/10.1002/ajmg.b.32240

25. Carlson, C. L., Pelham, W. E., Jr., Milich, R., & Dixon, J. (1992). Single and combined effects of methylphenidate and behavior therapy on the classroom performance of children with attention-deficit hyperactivity disorder. J Abnorm Child Psychol, 20(2), 213-232. https://doi.org/10.1007/bf00916549

26. Carlson, G. A., & Klein, D. N. (2020). Editorial: Antidepressants to the Rescue in Severe Mood Dysregulation and Disruptive Mood Dysregulation Disorder? J Am Acad Child Adolesc Psychiatry, 59(3), 339-341. https://doi.org/10.1016/j.jaac.2019.05.016

27. Carter, C. M., Urbanowicz, M., Hemsley, R., Mantilla, L., Strobel, S., Graham, P. J., & Taylor, E. (1993). Effects of a few food diet in attention deficit disorder. Arch Dis Child, 69(5), 564-568. https://doi.org/10.1136/adc.69.5.564

28. Centers for Disease Control and Prevention (CDC). (2005). Mental health in the United States. Prevalence of diagnosis and medication treatment for attention-deficit/hyperactivity disorder--United States, 2003. MMWR Morb Mortal Wkly Rep, 54(34), 842-847.

29. Chang, Z., D'Onofrio, B. M., Quinn, P. D., Lichtenstein, P., & Larsson, H. (2016). Medication for Attention-Deficit/Hyperactivity Disorder and Risk for Depression: A Nationwide Longitudinal Cohort Study. Biol Psychiatry, 80(12), 916-922. https://doi.org/10.1016/j.biopsych.2016.02.018

30. Chang, Z., Lichtenstein, P., D'Onofrio, B. M., Sjölander, A., & Larsson, H. (2014). Serious transport accidents in adults with attention-deficit/hyperactivity disorder and the effect of medication: a population-based study. JAMA Psychiatry, 71(3), 319-325. https://doi.org/10.1001/jamapsychiatry.2013.4174

31. Chang, Z., Lichtenstein, P., Långström, N., Larsson, H., & Fazel, S. (2016). Association Between Prescription of Major Psychotropic Medications and Violent Reoffending After Prison Release. Jama, 316(17), 1798-1807. https://doi.org/10.1001/jama.2016.15380

32. Chang, Z., Quinn, P. D., Hur, K., Gibbons, R. D., Sjölander, A., Larsson, H., & D'Onofrio, B. M. (2017). Association Between Medication Use for Attention-Deficit/Hyperactivity Disorder and Risk of Motor Vehicle Crashes. JAMA Psychiatry, 74(6), 597-603. https://doi.org/10.1001/jamapsychiatry.2017.0659

33. Charach, A., Carson, P., Fox, S., Ali, M. U., Beckett, J., & Lim, C. G. (2013). Interventions for preschool children at high risk for ADHD: a comparative effectiveness review. Pediatrics, 131(5), e1584-1604. https://doi.org/10.1542/peds.2012-0974

34. Chasle, V., Riffaud, L., Longuet, R., Martineau-Curt, M., Collet, Y., Le Fournier, L., & Pladys, P. (2016). Mild head injury and attention deficit hyperactivity disorder in children. Childs Nerv Syst, 32(12), 2357-2361. https://doi.org/10.1007/s00381-016-3230-z

35. Coghill, D. R., Caballero, B., Sorooshian, S., & Civil, R. (2014). A systematic review of the safety of lisdexamfetamine dimesylate. CNS Drugs, 28(6), 497-511. https://doi.org/10.1007/s40263-014-0166-2

36. Connor, D. F., Findling, R. L., Kollins, S. H., Sallee, F., López, F. A., Lyne, A., & Tremblay, G. (2010). Effects of guanfacine extended release on oppositional symptoms in children aged 6-12 years with attention-deficit hyperactivity disorder and oppositional symptoms: a randomized, double-blind, placebo-controlled trial. CNS Drugs, 24(9), 755-768. https://doi.org/10.2165/11537790-000000000-00000

37. Connor, D. F., Glatt, S. J., Lopez, I. D., Jackson, D., & Melloni, R. H., Jr. (2002). Psychopharmacology and aggression. I: A meta-analysis of stimulant effects on overt/covert aggression-related behaviors in ADHD. J Am Acad Child Adolesc Psychiatry, 41(3), 253-261. https://doi.org/10.1097/00004583-200203000-00004

38. Cortese, S., Adamo, N., Del Giovane, C., Mohr-Jensen, C., Hayes, A. J., Carucci, S., Atkinson, L. Z., Tessari, L., Banaschewski, T., Coghill, D., Hollis, C., Simonoff, E., Zuddas, A., Barbui, C., Purgato, M., Steinhausen, H. C., Shokraneh, F., Xia, J., & Cipriani, A. (2018). Comparative efficacy and tolerability of medications for attention-deficit hyperactivity disorder in children, adolescents, and adults: a systematic review and network meta-analysis. Lancet Psychiatry, 5(9), 727-738. https://doi.org/10.1016/s2215-0366(18)30269-4

39. Cortese, S., Holtmann, M., Banaschewski, T., Buitelaar, J., Coghill, D., Danckaerts, M., Dittmann, R. W., Graham, J., Taylor, E., & Sergeant, J. (2013). Practitioner review: current best practice in the management of adverse events during treatment with ADHD medications in children and

adolescents. J Child Psychol Psychiatry, 54(3), 227-246. https://doi.org/10.1111/jcpp.12036

40. Cortese, S., Moreira-Maia, C. R., St Fleur, D., Morcillo-Peñalver, C., Rohde, L. A., & Faraone, S. V. (2016). Association Between ADHD and Obesity: A Systematic Review and Meta-Analysis. Am J Psychiatry, 173(1), 34-43. https://doi.org/10.1176/appi.ajp.2015.15020266

41. Cotman, C. W., Berchtold, N. C., & Christie, L. A. (2007). Exercise builds brain health: key roles of growth factor cascades and inflammation. Trends Neurosci, 30(9), 464-472. https://doi.org/10.1016/j.tins.2007.06.011

42. Creer, D. J., Romberg, C., Saksida, L. M., van Praag, H., & Bussey, T. J. (2010). Running enhances spatial pattern separation in mice. Proc Natl Acad Sci U S A, 107(5), 2367-2372. https://doi.org/10.1073/pnas.0911725107

43. Cuffe, S. P., Visser, S. N., Holbrook, J. R., Danielson, M. L., Geryk, L. L., Wolraich, M. L., & McKeown, R. E. (2020). ADHD and Psychiatric Comorbidity: Functional Outcomes in a School-Based Sample of Children. J Atten Disord, 24(9), 1345-1354. https://doi.org/10.1177/1087054715613437

44. Dalsgaard, S., Leckman, J. F., Mortensen, P. B., Nielsen, H. S., & Simonsen, M. (2015). Effect of drugs on the risk of injuries in children with attention deficit hyperactivity disorder: a prospective cohort study. Lancet Psychiatry, 2(8), 702-709. https://doi.org/10.1016/s2215-0366(15)00271-0

45. Danielson, M. L., Bitsko, R. H., Ghandour, R. M., Holbrook, J. R., Kogan, M. D., & Blumberg, S. J. (2018). Prevalence of Parent-Reported ADHD Diagnosis and Associated Treatment Among U.S. Children and

Adolescents, 2016. J Clin Child Adolesc Psychol, 47(2), 199-212. https://doi.org/10.1080/15374416.2017.1417860

46. Donzelli, G., Carducci, A., Llopis-Gonzalez, A., Verani, M., Llopis-Morales, A., Cioni, L., & Morales-Suárez-Varela, M. (2019). The Association between Lead and Attention-Deficit/Hyperactivity Disorder: A Systematic Review. Int J Environ Res Public Health, 16(3). https://doi.org/10.3390/ijerph16030382

47. Drabick, D. A., Bubier, J., Chen, D., Price, J., & Lanza, H. I. (2011). Source-specific oppositional defiant disorder among inner-city children: prospective prediction and moderation. J Clin Child Adolesc Psychol, 40(1), 23-35. https://doi.org/10.1080/15374416.2011.533401

48. Dulcan, M. (1997). Practice parameters for the assessment and treatment of children, adolescents, and adults with attention-deficit/hyperactivity disorder. American Academy of Child and Adolescent Psychiatry. J Am Acad Child Adolesc Psychiatry, 36(10 Suppl), 85s-121s. https://doi.org/10.1097/00004583-199710001-00007

49. Dunn, G. A., Nigg, J. T., & Sullivan, E. L. (2019). Neuroinflammation as a risk factor for attention deficit hyperactivity disorder. Pharmacol Biochem Behav, 182, 22-34. https://doi.org/10.1016/j.pbb.2019.05.005

50. Egger, J., Carter, C. M., Graham, P. J., Gumley, D., & Soothill, J. F. (1985). Controlled trial of oligoantigenic treatment in the hyperkinetic syndrome. Lancet, 1(8428), 540-545. https://doi.org/10.1016/s0140-6736(85)91206-1

51. Egger, J., Stolla, A., & McEwen, L. M. (1992). Controlled trial of hyposensitisation in children with food-induced hyperkinetic syndrome. Lancet, 339(8802), 1150-1153. https://doi.org/10.1016/0140-6736(92)90742-1

52. Eichler, A., Hudler, L., Grunitz, J., Grimm, J., Raabe, E., Goecke, T. W., Fasching, P. A., Beckmann, M. W., Kratz, O., Moll, G. H., Kornhuber, J., & Heinrich, H. (2018). Effects of prenatal alcohol consumption on cognitive development and ADHD-related behaviour in primary-school age: a multilevel study based on meconium ethyl glucuronide. J Child Psychol Psychiatry, 59(2), 110-118. https://doi.org/10.1111/jcpp.12794

53. Elia, J., Ambrosini, P., & Berrettini, W. (2008). ADHD characteristics: I. Concurrent co-morbidity patterns in children & adolescents. Child Adolesc Psychiatry Ment Health, 2(1), 15. https://doi.org/10.1186/1753-2000-2-15

54. Elliott, R., Sahakian, B. J., Matthews, K., Bannerjea, A., Rimmer, J., & Robbins, T. W. (1997). Effects of methylphenidate on spatial working memory and planning in healthy young adults. Psychopharmacology (Berl), 131(2), 196-206. https://doi.org/10.1007/s002130050284

55. Erler, A. (2013). ADHD and stimulant drug treatment: what can the children teach us? J Med Ethics, 39(6), 357-358. https://doi.org/10.1136/medethics-2013-101562

56. Evans, S. W., Owens, J. S., Wymbs, B. T., & Ray, A. R. (2018). Evidence-Based Psychosocial Treatments for Children and Adolescents With Attention Deficit/Hyperactivity Disorder. J Clin Child Adolesc Psychol, 47(2), 157-198. https://doi.org/10.1080/15374416.2017.1390757

57. Fadus, M. C., Ginsburg, K. R., Sobowale, K., Halliday-Boykins, C. A., Bryant, B. E., Gray, K. M., & Squeglia, L. M. (2020). Unconscious Bias and the Diagnosis of Disruptive Behavior Disorders and ADHD in African American and Hispanic Youth. Acad Psychiatry, 44(1), 95-102. https://doi.org/10.1007/s40596-019-01127-6

58. Farah, M. J., Illes, J., Cook-Deegan, R., Gardner, H., Kandel, E., King, P., Parens, E., Sahakian, B., & Wolpe, P. R. (2004). Neurocognitive enhancement: what can we do and what should we do? Nat Rev Neurosci, 5(5), 421-425. https://doi.org/10.1038/nrn1390

59. Faraone, S. V., Asherson, P., Banaschewski, T., Biederman, J., Buitelaar, J. K., Ramos-Quiroga, J. A., Rohde, L. A., Sonuga-Barke, E. J., Tannock, R., & Franke, B. (2015). Attention-deficit/hyperactivity disorder. Nat Rev Dis Primers, 1, 15020. https://doi.org/10.1038/nrdp.2015.20

60. Faraone, S. V., & Biederman, J. (2016). Can Attention-Deficit/Hyperactivity Disorder Onset Occur in Adulthood? JAMA Psychiatry, 73(7), 655-656. https://doi.org/10.1001/jamapsychiatry.2016.0400

61. Faraone, S. V., Biederman, J., & Monuteaux, M. C. (2000). Toward guidelines for pedigree selection in genetic studies of attention deficit hyperactivity disorder. Genet Epidemiol, 18(1), 1-16. https://doi.org/10.1002/(sici)1098-2272(200001)18:1<1::Aid-gepi1>3.0.Co;2-x

62. Feldman, M. E., Charach, A., & Bélanger, S. A. (2018). ADHD in children and youth: Part 2-Treatment. Paediatr Child Health, 23(7), 462-472. https://doi.org/10.1093/pch/pxy113

63. Fliers, E. A., Buitelaar, J. K., Maras, A., Bul, K., Höhle, E., Faraone, S. V., Franke, B., & Rommelse, N. N. (2013). ADHD is a risk factor for overweight and obesity in children. J Dev Behav Pediatr, 34(8), 566-574. https://doi.org/10.1097/DBP.0b013e3182a50a67

64. Floet, A. M., Scheiner, C., & Grossman, L. (2010). Attention-deficit/hyperactivity disorder. Pediatr Rev, 31(2), 56-69. https://doi.org/10.1542/pir.31-2-56

65. Food Advisory Committee of the US FDA Quick Minutes: Food Advisory Committee Meeting March 30-31, 2011. www.fda.gov/AdvisoryCommittees/CommitteesMeetings Materials/FoodAdvisoryCommittee/ucm250901.htm

66. Franz, A. P., Bolat, G. U., Bolat, H., Matijasevich, A., Santos, I. S., Silveira, R. C., Procianoy, R. S., Rohde, L. A., & Moreira-Maia, C. R. (2018). Attention-Deficit/Hyperactivity Disorder and Very Preterm/Very Low Birth Weight: A Meta-analysis. Pediatrics, 141(1). https://doi.org/10.1542/peds.2017-1645

67. Froehlich, T. E., McGough, J. J., & Stein, M. A. (2010). Progress and promise of attention-deficit hyperactivity disorder pharmacogenetics. CNS Drugs, 24(2), 99-117. https://doi.org/10.2165/11530290-000000000-00000

68. Fuemmeler, B. F., Østbye, T., Yang, C., McClernon, F. J., & Kollins, S. H. (2011). Association between attention-deficit/hyperactivity disorder symptoms and obesity and hypertension in early adulthood: a population-based study. Int J Obes (Lond), 35(6), 852-862. https://doi.org/10.1038/ijo.2010.214

69. Gadow, K. D., Nolan, E. E., Litcher, L., Carlson, G. A., Panina, N., Golovakha, E., Sprafkin, J., & Bromet, E. J. (2000). Comparison of attention-deficit/hyperactivity disorder symptom subtypes in Ukrainian schoolchildren. J Am Acad Child Adolesc Psychiatry, 39(12), 1520-1527. https://doi.org/10.1097/00004583-200012000-00014

70. Gaub, M., & Carlson, C. L. (1997). Gender differences in ADHD: a meta-analysis and critical review. J Am Acad

Child Adolesc Psychiatry, 36(8), 1036-1045. https://doi.org/10.1097/00004583-199708000-00011

71. Geller, B., Warner, K., Williams, M., & Zimerman, B. (1998). Prepubertal and young adolescent bipolarity versus ADHD: assessment and validity using the WASH-U-KSADS, CBCL and TRF. J Affect Disord, 51(2), 93-100. https://doi.org/10.1016/s0165-0327(98)00176-1

72. Geller, B., Williams, M., Zimerman, B., Frazier, J., Beringer, L., & Warner, K. L. (1998). Prepubertal and early adolescent bipolarity differentiate from ADHD by manic symptoms, grandiose delusions, ultra-rapid or ultradian cycling. J Affect Disord, 51(2), 81-91. https://doi.org/10.1016/s0165-0327(98)00175-x

73. Getahun, D., Jacobsen, S. J., Fassett, M. J., Chen, W., Demissie, K., & Rhoads, G. G. (2013). Recent trends in childhood attention-deficit/hyperactivity disorder. JAMA Pediatr, 167(3), 282-288. https://doi.org/10.1001/2013.jamapediatrics.401

74. Ghirardi, L., Larsson, H., Chang, Z., Chen, Q., Quinn, P. D., Hur, K., Gibbons, R. D., & D'Onofrio, B. M. (2020). Attention-Deficit/Hyperactivity Disorder Medication and Unintentional Injuries in Children and Adolescents. J Am Acad Child Adolesc Psychiatry, 59(8), 944-951. https://doi.org/10.1016/j.jaac.2019.06.010

75. Gibbs, E. L., Kass, A. E., Eichen, D. M., Fitzsimmons-Craft, E. E., Trockel, M., & Wilfley, D. E. (2016). Attention-deficit/hyperactivity disorder-specific stimulant misuse, mood, anxiety, and stress in college-age women at high risk for or with eating disorders. J Am Coll Health, 64(4), 300-308. https://doi.org/10.1080/07448481.2016.1138477

76. Greenhill, L., Kollins, S., Abikoff, H., McCracken, J., Riddle, M., Swanson, J., McGough, J., Wigal, S., Wigal, T., Vitiello, B., Skrobala, A., Posner, K., Ghuman, J., Cunningham, C., Davies, M., Chuang, S., & Cooper, T. (2006). Efficacy and safety of immediate-release methylphenidate treatment for preschoolers with ADHD. J Am Acad Child Adolesc Psychiatry, 45(11), 1284-1293. https://doi.org/10.1097/01.chi.0000235077.32661.61

77. Greenhill, L. L., Swanson, J. M., Hechtman, L., Waxmonsky, J., Arnold, L. E., Molina, B. S. G., Hinshaw, S. P., Jensen, P. S., Abikoff, H. B., Wigal, T., Stehli, A., Howard, A., Hermanussen, M., & Hanć, T. (2020). Trajectories of Growth Associated With Long-Term Stimulant Medication in the Multimodal Treatment Study of Attention-Deficit/Hyperactivity Disorder. J Am Acad Child Adolesc Psychiatry, 59(8), 978-989. https://doi.org/10.1016/j.jaac.2019.06.019

78. Grigorenko, E. L. (2007). Learning Disabilities. In A. Martin, M. H. Bloch, & F. R. Volkmar (Eds.), Lewis's child and adolescent psychiatry : a comprehensive textbook (5th ed., pp. 444). Wolters Kluwer Health/Lippincott Williams & Wilkins.

79. Gustavson, K., Ystrom, E., Stoltenberg, C., Susser, E., Surén, P., Magnus, P., Knudsen, G. P., Smith, G. D., Langley, K., Rutter, M., Aase, H., & Reichborn-Kjennerud, T. (2017). Smoking in Pregnancy and Child ADHD. Pediatrics, 139(2). https://doi.org/10.1542/peds.2016-2509

80. Guttmann, E., & Sargant, W. (1937). Observations on Benzedrine. Br Med J, 1(3984), 1013-1015. https://doi.org/10.1136/bmj.1.3984.1013

81. Hammerness, P., McCarthy, K., Mancuso, E., Gendron, C., & Geller, D. (2009). Atomoxetine for the treatment of

attention-deficit/hyperactivity disorder in children and adolescents: a review. Neuropsychiatr Dis Treat, 5, 215-226. https://doi.org/10.2147/ndt.s3896

82. Hanć, T., & Cortese, S. (2018). Attention deficit/hyperactivity-disorder and obesity: A review and model of current hypotheses explaining their comorbidity. Neurosci Biobehav Rev, 92, 16-28. https://doi.org/10.1016/j.neubiorev.2018.05.017

83. Harrison, A. G., Edwards, M. J., & Parker, K. C. (2007). Identifying students faking ADHD: Preliminary findings and strategies for detection. Arch Clin Neuropsychol, 22(5), 577-588. https://doi.org/10.1016/j.acn.2007.03.008

84. Harrison, J., Bunford, N., Evans, S., & Owens, J. (2013). Educational accommodations for students with behavioral challenges: a systematic review of the literature. Rev Educ Res, 83(4), 551-597.

85. Harstad, E., & Levy, S. (2014). Attention-deficit/hyperactivity disorder and substance abuse. Pediatrics, 134(1), e293-301. https://doi.org/10.1542/peds.2014-0992

86. Harstad, E. B., Weaver, A. L., Katusic, S. K., Colligan, R. C., Kumar, S., Chan, E., Voigt, R. G., & Barbaresi, W. J. (2014). ADHD, stimulant treatment, and growth: a longitudinal study. Pediatrics, 134(4), e935-944. https://doi.org/10.1542/peds.2014-0428

87. Harvey, E. A., Youngwirth, S. D., Thakar, D. A., & Errazuriz, P. A. (2009). Predicting attention-deficit/hyperactivity disorder and oppositional defiant disorder from preschool diagnostic assessments. J Consult Clin Psychol, 77(2), 349-354. https://doi.org/10.1037/a0014638

88. Heal, D. J., Smith, S. L., Gosden, J., & Nutt, D. J. (2013). Amphetamine, past and present--a pharmacological and clinical perspective. J Psychopharmacol, 27(6), 479-496. https://doi.org/10.1177/0269881113482532

89. Henry, N., Moffitt, T.E., Caspi, A., Langley, J., Silva, J.M. (1994). On the "remembrance of things past": A longitudinal evaluations of the retrospective method.

90. . Psychological Assessment, 6, 92-101.

91. Heyn, P., Abreu, B. C., & Ottenbacher, K. J. (2004). The effects of exercise training on elderly persons with cognitive impairment and dementia: a meta-analysis. Arch Phys Med Rehabil, 85(10), 1694-1704. https://doi.org/10.1016/j.apmr.2004.03.019

92. Hillman, C. H., Erickson, K. I., & Kramer, A. F. (2008). Be smart, exercise your heart: exercise effects on brain and cognition. Nat Rev Neurosci, 9(1), 58-65. https://doi.org/10.1038/nrn2298

93. Hinshaw, S. P., & Scheffler, R. M. (2014). The ADHD explosion myths, medication, money, and today's push for performance. Oxford University Press.

94. Hirota, T., Schwartz, S., & Correll, C. U. (2014). Alpha-2 agonists for attention-deficit/hyperactivity disorder in youth: a systematic review and meta-analysis of monotherapy and add-on trials to stimulant therapy. J Am Acad Child Adolesc Psychiatry, 53(2), 153-173. https://doi.org/10.1016/j.jaac.2013.11.009

95. Holbrook, J. R., Bitsko, R. H., Danielson, M. L., & Visser, S. N. (2017). Interpreting the Prevalence of Mental Disorders in Children: Tribulation and Triangulation. Health Promot Pract, 18(1), 5-7. https://doi.org/10.1177/1524839916677730

96. Huang, L., Wang, Y., Zhang, L., Zheng, Z., Zhu, T., Qu, Y., & Mu, D. (2018). Maternal Smoking and Attention-Deficit/Hyperactivity Disorder in Offspring: A Meta-analysis. Pediatrics, 141(1). https://doi.org/10.1542/peds.2017-2465

97. Jeffers, A., Benotsch, E. G., & Koester, S. (2013). Misuse of prescription stimulants for weight loss, psychosocial variables, and eating disordered behaviors. Appetite, 65, 8-13. https://doi.org/10.1016/j.appet.2013.01.008

98. Jeffers, A. J., & Benotsch, E. G. (2014). Non-medical use of prescription stimulants for weight loss, disordered eating, and body image. Eat Behav, 15(3), 414-418. https://doi.org/10.1016/j.eatbeh.2014.04.019

99. Jensen, P. S., Hinshaw, S. P., Swanson, J. M., Greenhill, L. L., Conners, C. K., Arnold, L. E., Abikoff, H. B., Elliott, G., Hechtman, L., Hoza, B., March, J. S., Newcorn, J. H., Severe, J. B., Vitiello, B., Wells, K., & Wigal, T. (2001). Findings from the NIMH Multimodal Treatment Study of ADHD (MTA): implications and applications for primary care providers. J Dev Behav Pediatr, 22(1), 60-73. https://doi.org/10.1097/00004703-200102000-00008

100. Joensen, B., Meyer, M., & Aagaard, L. (2017). Specific Genes Associated with Adverse Events of Methylphenidate Use in the Pediatric Population: A Systematic Literature Review. J Res Pharm Pract, 6(2), 65-72. https://doi.org/10.4103/jrpp.JRPP_16_161

101. Kambeitz, J., Romanos, M., & Ettinger, U. (2014). Meta-analysis of the association between dopamine transporter genotype and response to methylphenidate treatment in ADHD. Pharmacogenomics J, 14(1), 77-84. https://doi.org/10.1038/tpj.2013.9

102. Kaplan, A., & Adesman, A. (2011). Clinical diagnosis and management of attention deficit hyperactivity disorder in preschool children. Curr Opin Pediatr, 23(6), 684-692. https://doi.org/10.1097/MOP.0b013e32834cbbba

103. Karasu, S. R. (2017). Psychoanalysis and Psychoanalytic Psychotherapy. In B. J. Sadock, V. A. Sadock, & P. Ruiz (Eds.), Kaplan and Sadock's comprehensive textbook of psychiatry (10th ed., pp. 2638). Wolters Kluwer Health/Lippincott Williams & Wilkins.

104. Keenan, K., & Wakschlag, L. S. (2000). More than the terrible twos: the nature and severity of behavior problems in clinic-referred preschool children. J Abnorm Child Psychol, 28(1), 33-46. https://doi.org/10.1023/a:1005118000977

105. Kessler, R. C., Adler, L. A., Barkley, R., Biederman, J., Conners, C. K., Faraone, S. V., Greenhill, L. L., Jaeger, S., Secnik, K., Spencer, T., Ustün, T. B., & Zaslavsky, A. M. (2005). Patterns and predictors of attention-deficit/hyperactivity disorder persistence into adulthood: results from the national comorbidity survey replication. Biol Psychiatry, 57(11), 1442-1451. https://doi.org/10.1016/j.biopsych.2005.04.001

106. Kessler, R. C., Amminger, G. P., Aguilar-Gaxiola, S., Alonso, J., Lee, S., & Ustün, T. B. (2007). Age of onset of mental disorders: a review of recent literature. Curr Opin Psychiatry, 20(4), 359-364. https://doi.org/10.1097/YCO.0b013e32816ebc8c

107. Kieling, C., Genro, J. P., Hutz, M. H., & Rohde, L. A. (2010). A current update on ADHD pharmacogenomics. Pharmacogenomics, 11(3), 407-419. https://doi.org/10.2217/pgs.10.28

108. Kolko, D. J., Bukstein, O. G., & Barron, J. (1999). Methylphenidate and behavior modification in children with ADHD and comorbid ODD or CD: main and incremental effects across settings. J Am Acad Child Adolesc Psychiatry, 38(5), 578-586. https://doi.org/10.1097/00004583-199905000-00020

109. Korrel, H., Mueller, K. L., Silk, T., Anderson, V., & Sciberras, E. (2017). Research Review: Language problems in children with Attention-Deficit Hyperactivity Disorder - a systematic meta-analytic review. J Child Psychol Psychiatry, 58(6), 640-654. https://doi.org/10.1111/jcpp.12688

110. Kraft, G. H., & Bowen, J. (2005). Modafinil for fatigue in MS: a randomized placebo-controlled double-blind study. Neurology, 65(12), 1995-1997; author reply 1995-1997. https://doi.org/10.1212/01.wnl.0000200985.04239.53

111. Kramer, J. R., Loney, J., Ponto, L. B., Roberts, M. A., & Grossman, S. (2000). Predictors of adult height and weight in boys treated with methylphenidate for childhood behavior problems. J Am Acad Child Adolesc Psychiatry, 39(4), 517-524. https://doi.org/10.1097/00004583-200004000-00022

112. Krull, K. R. (2022a). ADHD in children and adolescents: Overview of treatment and prognosis. In M. Augustyn, Torchia M.M. (Ed.), UpToDate. Wolters Kluver.

113. Krull, K. R. (2022b). Attention deficit hyperactivity disorder in children and adolescents: Epidemiology and pathogenesis. In M. Augustyn, Torchia M.M. (Ed.), UpToDate. Wolters Kluwer.

114. Lahey, B. B., Pelham, W. E., Stein, M. A., Loney, J., Trapani, C., Nugent, K., Kipp, H., Schmidt, E., Lee, S., Cale, M., Gold, E., Hartung, C. M., Willcutt, E., &

Baumann, B. (1998). Validity of DSM-IV attention-deficit/hyperactivity disorder for younger children. J Am Acad Child Adolesc Psychiatry, 37(7), 695-702. https://doi.org/10.1097/00004583-199807000-00008

115. Langberg, J. M., Molina, B. S., Arnold, L. E., Epstein, J. N., Altaye, M., Hinshaw, S. P., Swanson, J. M., Wigal, T., & Hechtman, L. (2011). Patterns and predictors of adolescent academic achievement and performance in a sample of children with attention-deficit/hyperactivity disorder. J Clin Child Adolesc Psychol, 40(4), 519-531. https://doi.org/10.1080/15374416.2011.581620

116. Layton, T. J., Barnett, M. L., Hicks, T. R., & Jena, A. B. (2018). Attention Deficit-Hyperactivity Disorder and Month of School Enrollment. N Engl J Med, 379(22), 2122-2130. https://doi.org/10.1056/NEJMoa1806828

117. Levy, F., Hay, D. A., McStephen, M., Wood, C., & Waldman, I. (1997). Attention-deficit hyperactivity disorder: a category or a continuum? Genetic analysis of a large-scale twin study. J Am Acad Child Adolesc Psychiatry, 36(6), 737-744. https://doi.org/10.1097/00004583-199706000-00009

118. Lichtenstein, P., Halldner, L., Zetterqvist, J., Sjölander, A., Serlachius, E., Fazel, S., Långström, N., & Larsson, H. (2012). Medication for attention deficit-hyperactivity disorder and criminality. N Engl J Med, 367(21), 2006-2014. https://doi.org/10.1056/NEJMoa1203241

119. Lindemann, C., Langner, I., Banaschewski, T., Garbe, E., & Mikolajczyk, R. T. (2017). The Risk of Hospitalizations with Injury Diagnoses in a Matched Cohort of Children and Adolescents with and without Attention Deficit/Hyperactivity Disorder in Germany: A Database Study. Front Pediatr, 5, 220. https://doi.org/10.3389/fped.2017.00220

120. Man, K. K. C., Ip, P., Chan, E., & al., e. (2017). Attention-Deficit/ Hyperactivity Disorder (ADHD) Drug Prescribing Trend is Increasing Among School-aged Children and Adolescents. J Atten Disord, 37(9), 711-721.

121. Mannuzza, S., Klein, R. G., Bessler, A., Malloy, P., & LaPadula, M. (1993). Adult outcome of hyperactive boys. Educational achievement, occupational rank, and psychiatric status. Arch Gen Psychiatry, 50(7), 565-576. https://doi.org/10.1001/archpsyc.1993.01820190067007

122. Mannuzza, S., Klein, R. G., Bessler, A., Malloy, P., & LaPadula, M. (1998). Adult psychiatric status of hyperactive boys grown up. Am J Psychiatry, 155(4), 493-498. https://doi.org/10.1176/ajp.155.4.493

123. Mannuzza, S., Klein, R. G., Klein, D. F., Bessler, A., & Shrout, P. (2002). Accuracy of adult recall of childhood attention deficit hyperactivity disorder. Am J Psychiatry, 159(11), 1882-1888. https://doi.org/10.1176/appi.ajp.159.11.1882

124. Marcus, D. (2002). Neuroethics : Mapping the Field Conference Proceedings, 13-14 May, 2002, San Francisco, California. The Dana Press.

125. Markowitz, J. S., & Patrick, K. S. (2017). The Clinical Pharmacokinetics of Amphetamines Utilized in the Treatment of Attention-Deficit/Hyperactivity Disorder. J Child Adolesc Psychopharmacol, 27(8), 678-689. https://doi.org/10.1089/cap.2017.0071

126. Max, J. E., Koele, S. L., Smith, W. L., Jr., Sato, Y., Lindgren, S. D., Robin, D. A., & Arndt, S. (1998). Psychiatric disorders in children and adolescents after severe traumatic brain injury: a controlled study. J Am Acad Child Adolesc Psychiatry, 37(8), 832-840. https://doi.org/10.1097/00004583-199808000-00013

127. Mayes, R., Bagwell, C., & Erkulwater, J. (2008). ADHD and the rise in stimulant use among children. Harv Rev Psychiatry, 16(3), 151-166. https://doi.org/10.1080/10673220802167782

128. Michelson, D., Allen, A. J., Busner, J., Casat, C., Dunn, D., Kratochvil, C., Newcorn, J., Sallee, F. R., Sangal, R. B., Saylor, K., West, S., Kelsey, D., Wernicke, J., Trapp, N. J., & Harder, D. (2002). Once-daily atomoxetine treatment for children and adolescents with attention deficit hyperactivity disorder: a randomized, placebo-controlled study. Am J Psychiatry, 159(11), 1896-1901. https://doi.org/10.1176/appi.ajp.159.11.1896

129. Michelson, D., Faries, D., Wernicke, J., Kelsey, D., Kendrick, K., Sallee, F. R., & Spencer, T. (2001). Atomoxetine in the treatment of children and adolescents with attention-deficit/hyperactivity disorder: a randomized, placebo-controlled, dose-response study. Pediatrics, 108(5), E83. https://doi.org/10.1542/peds.108.5.e83

130. Mikolajczyk, R., Horn, J., Schmedt, N., Langner, I., Lindemann, C., & Garbe, E. (2015). Injury prevention by medication among children with attention-deficit/hyperactivity disorder: a case-only study. JAMA Pediatr, 169(4), 391-395. https://doi.org/10.1001/jamapediatrics.2014.3275

131. Millichap, J. G., & Yee, M. M. (2012). The diet factor in attention-deficit/hyperactivity disorder. Pediatrics, 129(2), 330-337. https://doi.org/10.1542/peds.2011-2199

132. Minzenberg, M. J., & Carter, C. S. (2008). Modafinil: a review of neurochemical actions and effects on cognition. Neuropsychopharmacology, 33(7), 1477-1502. https://doi.org/10.1038/sj.npp.1301534

133. Moffitt, T. E., Houts, R., Asherson, P., Belsky, D. W., Corcoran, D. L., Hammerle, M., Harrington, H., Hogan, S., Meier, M. H., Polanczyk, G. V., Poulton, R., Ramrakha, S., Sugden, K., Williams, B., Rohde, L. A., & Caspi, A. (2015). Is Adult ADHD a Childhood-Onset Neurodevelopmental Disorder? Evidence From a Four-Decade Longitudinal Cohort Study. Am J Psychiatry, 172(10), 967-977. https://doi.org/10.1176/appi.ajp.2015.14101266

134. Mohamed, A. D., & Sahakian, B. J. (2012). The ethics of elective psychopharmacology. Int J Neuropsychopharmacol, 15(4), 559-571. https://doi.org/10.1017/s146114571100037x

135. Morein-Zamir, S., Robbins, T.W., Turner, D., Sahakian, B.J.,. (2008). State-of-science review: SR-E9: pharamcological cognitive enhancement. In Mental Capital and Wellbeing: Making the Most of Ourselves in the 21st Century (pp. 3-16). Foresight Mental Capital and Wellbeing Project. .

136. Mosholder, A. D., Gelperin, K., Hammad, T. A., Phelan, K., & Johann-Liang, R. (2009). Hallucinations and other psychotic symptoms associated with the use of attention-deficit/hyperactivity disorder drugs in children. Pediatrics, 123(2), 611-616. https://doi.org/10.1542/peds.2008-0185

137. MTA Cooperative Group. (1999). A 14-month randomized clinical trial of treatment strategies for attention-deficit/hyperactivity disorder. The MTA Cooperative Group. Multimodal Treatment Study of Children with ADHD. Arch Gen Psychiatry, 56(12), 1073-1086. https://doi.org/10.1001/archpsyc.56.12.1073

138. Mueller, K. L., & Tomblin, J. B. (2012). Examining the comorbidity of language disorders and ADHD. Top Lang

Disord, 32(3), 228-246.
https://doi.org/10.1097/TLD.0b013e318262010d

139. Mulraney, M., Schilpzand, E. J., Hazell, P., Nicholson, J.
M., Anderson, V., Efron, D., Silk, T. J., & Sciberras, E.
(2016). Comorbidity and correlates of disruptive mood
dysregulation disorder in 6-8-year-old children with
ADHD. Eur Child Adolesc Psychiatry, 25(3), 321-330.
https://doi.org/10.1007/s00787-015-0738-9

140. Nasser, A., Liranso, T., Adewole, T., Fry, N., Hull, J. T.,
Chowdhry, F., Busse, G. D., Cutler, A. J., Jones, N. J.,
Findling, R. L., & Schwabe, S. (2020). A Phase III,
Randomized, Placebo-controlled Trial to Assess the
Efficacy and Safety of Once-daily SPN-812 (Viloxazine
Extended-release) in the Treatment of Attention-
deficit/Hyperactivity Disorder in School-age Children.
Clin Ther, 42(8), 1452-1466.
https://doi.org/10.1016/j.clinthera.2020.05.021

141. National Institute for Health and Care Excellence (2018).
National Institute for Health and Care Excellence:
Guidelines. In Attention deficit hyperactivity disorder:
diagnosis and management. National Institute for Health
and Care Excellence (NICE)

Copyright © NICE 2018.

142. Newcorn, J. H., Spencer, T. J., Biederman, J., Milton, D.
R., & Michelson, D. (2005). Atomoxetine treatment in
children and adolescents with attention-
deficit/hyperactivity disorder and comorbid oppositional
defiant disorder. J Am Acad Child Adolesc Psychiatry,
44(3), 240-248. https://doi.org/10.1097/00004583-
200503000-00008

143. Newcorn, J. H., Sutton, V. K., Weiss, M. D., & Sumner, C.
R. (2009). Clinical responses to atomoxetine in attention-

deficit/hyperactivity disorder: the Integrated Data Exploratory Analysis (IDEA) study. J Am Acad Child Adolesc Psychiatry, 48(5), 511-518. https://doi.org/10.1097/CHI.0b013e31819c55b2

144. Nieves, A. V., & Lang, A. E. (2002). Treatment of excessive daytime sleepiness in patients with Parkinson's disease with modafinil. Clin Neuropharmacol, 25(2), 111-114. https://doi.org/10.1097/00002826-200203000-00010

145. Nigg, J. T., Johnstone, J. M., Musser, E. D., Long, H. G., Willoughby, M. T., & Shannon, J. (2016). Attention-deficit/hyperactivity disorder (ADHD) and being overweight/obesity: New data and meta-analysis. Clin Psychol Rev, 43, 67-79. https://doi.org/10.1016/j.cpr.2015.11.005

146. Nussey, C., Pistrang, N., & Murphy, T. (2013). How does psychoeducation help? A review of the effects of providing information about Tourette syndrome and attention-deficit/hyperactivity disorder. Child Care Health Dev, 39(5), 617-627. https://doi.org/10.1111/cch.12039

147. Nutley, S. K., Mathews, C. A., & Striley, C. W. (2020). Disordered eating is associated with non-medical use of prescription stimulants among college students. Drug Alcohol Depend, 209, 107907. https://doi.org/10.1016/j.drugalcdep.2020.107907

148. Owen, A. M., Downes, J. J., Sahakian, B. J., Polkey, C. E., & Robbins, T. W. (1990). Planning and spatial working memory following frontal lobe lesions in man. Neuropsychologia, 28(10), 1021-1034. https://doi.org/10.1016/0028-3932(90)90137-d

149. Pavuluri, M. N., Luk, S. L., & McGee, R. (1999). Parent reported preschool attention deficit hyperactivity:

measurement and validity. Eur Child Adolesc Psychiatry, 8(2), 126-133. https://doi.org/10.1007/s007870050093

150. Pediatrics. Subcomittee on ADHD. (2011). ADHD: clinical practice guideline for the diagnosis, evaluation, and treatment of attention-deficit/hyperactivity disorder in children and adolescents. Pediatrics, 128(5), 1007-1022. https://doi.org/10.1542/peds.2011-2654

151. Pelham, W. E., Jr., & Fabiano, G. A. (2008). Evidence-based psychosocial treatments for attention-deficit/hyperactivity disorder. J Clin Child Adolesc Psychol, 37(1), 184-214. https://doi.org/10.1080/15374410701818681

152. Pelham, W. E., Jr., Wheeler, T., & Chronis, A. (1998). Empirically supported psychosocial treatments for attention deficit hyperactivity disorder. J Clin Child Psychol, 27(2), 190-205. https://doi.org/10.1207/s15374424jccp2702_6

153. Pennington, B. F., & Ozonoff, S. (1996). Executive functions and developmental psychopathology. J Child Psychol Psychiatry, 37(1), 51-87. https://doi.org/10.1111/j.1469-7610.1996.tb01380.x

154. Petti, T. A. (2022). Communication Disorders, Spericific Learning Disoder, and Motor Disorder. In M. Dulcan (Ed.), Dulcan's Textbook of Child and Adolescent Psychiatry (Third ed., pp. 165). American Psychiatric Association Publishing.

155. Pliszka, S. R. (2022). Attention-Deficit/ Hyperactivity Disorder. In M. Dulcan (Ed.), Dulcan's Textbook of Child and Adolescent Psychiatry (Third ed., pp. 173-195). American Psychiatric Association Publishing.

156. Poblano, A., & Romero, E. (2006). ECI-4 screening of attention deficit-hyperactivity disorder and co-morbidity in

Mexican preschool children: preliminary results. Arq Neuropsiquiatr, 64(4), 932-936. https://doi.org/10.1590/s0004-282x2006000600008

157. President's Council on Bioethics (2003). Beyond therapy : biotechnology and the pursuit of human improvement. http://www.bioethics.gov/background/kasspaper.html

158. Quinn, P. D., Chang, Z., Hur, K., Gibbons, R. D., Lahey, B. B., Rickert, M. E., Sjölander, A., Lichtenstein, P., Larsson, H., & D'Onofrio, B. M. (2017). ADHD Medication and Substance-Related Problems. Am J Psychiatry, 174(9), 877-885. https://doi.org/10.1176/appi.ajp.2017.16060686

159. Raman, S. R., Man, K. K. C., Bahmanyar, S., Berard, A., Bilder, S., Boukhris, T., Bushnell, G., Crystal, S., Furu, K., KaoYang, Y. H., Karlstad, Ø., Kieler, H., Kubota, K., Lai, E. C., Martikainen, J. E., Maura, G., Moore, N., Montero, D., Nakamura, H., . . . Wong, I. C. K. (2018). Trends in attention-deficit hyperactivity disorder medication use: a retrospective observational study using population-based databases. Lancet Psychiatry, 5(10), 824-835. https://doi.org/10.1016/s2215-0366(18)30293-1

160. Raman, S. R., Marshall, S. W., Haynes, K., Gaynes, B. N., Naftel, A. J., & Stürmer, T. (2013). Stimulant treatment and injury among children with attention deficit hyperactivity disorder: an application of the self-controlled case series study design. Inj Prev, 19(3), 164-170. https://doi.org/10.1136/injuryprev-2012-040483

161. Randall, K. (2004). Mentally ill inmate put to death after medical 'treatment' prepares execution. http://www.cognitiveliberty.org/dll/singleton_executed.html

162. Rojas, N. L., & Chan, E. (2005). Old and new controversies in the alternative treatment of attention-deficit hyperactivity disorder. Ment Retard Dev Disabil Res Rev, 11(2), 116-130. https://doi.org/10.1002/mrdd.20064

163. Ruiz-Goikoetxea, M., Cortese, S., Aznarez-Sanado, M., Magallon, S., Alvarez Zallo, N., Luis, E. O., de Castro-Manglano, P., Soutullo, C., & Arrondo, G. (2018). Risk of unintentional injuries in children and adolescents with ADHD and the impact of ADHD medications: A systematic review and meta-analysis. Neurosci Biobehav Rev, 84, 63-71. https://doi.org/10.1016/j.neubiorev.2017.11.007

164. Sadock, B. J., Sadock, V. A., & Ruiz, P. (2017). Kaplan & Sadock's comprehensive textbook of psychiatry (10th ed.). Wolters Kluwer Health/Lippincott Williams & Wilkins.

165. Sadock, B. J., Sadock, V. A., Ruiz, P., & Kaplan, H. I. (2011). Kaplan and Sadock's comprehensive textbook of psychiatry, 9th edition (9th ed.). Westlaw.

166. Sahakian, B., & Morein-Zamir, S. (2007). Professor's little helper. Nature, 450(7173), 1157-1159. https://doi.org/10.1038/4501157a

167. Sahakian, B. J., Malloch, G., & Kennard, C. (2010). A UK strategy for mental health and wellbeing. Lancet, 375(9729), 1854-1855. https://doi.org/10.1016/s0140-6736(10)60817-3

168. Sahakian, B. J., & Morein-Zamir, S. (2011). Neuroethical issues in cognitive enhancement. J Psychopharmacol, 25(2), 197-204. https://doi.org/10.1177/0269881109106926

169. Salkever, D. S. (1995). Updated estimates of earnings benefits from reduced exposure of children to

environmental lead. Environ Res, 70(1), 1-6.
https://doi.org/10.1006/enrs.1995.1038

170. Satterfield, J. H., Cantwell, D. P., Schell, A., & Blaschke, T. (1979). Growth of hyperactive children treated with methylphenidate. Arch Gen Psychiatry, 36(2), 212-217. https://doi.org/10.1001/archpsyc.1979.01780020102011

171. Savulescu, J. (2006). Justice, fairness, and enhancement. Ann N Y Acad Sci, 1093, 321-338. https://doi.org/10.1196/annals.1382.021

172. Schechter, J. C., & Kollins, S. H. (2017). Prenatal Smoke Exposure and ADHD: Advancing the Field. Pediatrics, 139(2). https://doi.org/10.1542/peds.2016-3481

173. Schmidt, M. H., Möcks, P., Lay, B., Eisert, H. G., Fojkar, R., Fritz-Sigmund, D., Marcus, A., & Musaeus, B. (1997). Does oligoantigenic diet influence hyperactive/conduct-disordered children--a controlled trial. Eur Child Adolesc Psychiatry, 6(2), 88-95. https://doi.org/10.1007/bf00566671

174. Schwartz, J. (1994). Low-level lead exposure and children's IQ: a meta-analysis and search for a threshold. Environ Res, 65(1), 42-55. https://doi.org/10.1006/enrs.1994.1020

175. Schwarz, A. (2016). ADHD nation: children, doctors, big pharma, and the making of an American epidemic. Simon and Schuster.

176. Shaw, M., Hodgkins, P., Caci, H., Young, S., Kahle, J., Woods, A. G., & Arnold, L. E. (2012). A systematic review and analysis of long-term outcomes in attention deficit hyperactivity disorder: effects of treatment and non-treatment. BMC Med, 10, 99. https://doi.org/10.1186/1741-7015-10-99

177. Shaw, P., Stringaris, A., Nigg, J., & Leibenluft, E. (2014). Emotion dysregulation in attention deficit hyperactivity disorder. Am J Psychiatry, 171(3), 276-293. https://doi.org/10.1176/appi.ajp.2013.13070966

178. Shearer, J., Darke, S., Rodgers, C., Slade, T., van Beek, I., Lewis, J., Brady, D., McKetin, R., Mattick, R. P., & Wodak, A. (2009). A double-blind, placebo-controlled trial of modafinil (200 mg/day) for methamphetamine dependence. Addiction, 104(2), 224-233. https://doi.org/10.1111/j.1360-0443.2008.02437.x

179. Sibley, M. H., Graziano, P. A., Kuriyan, A. B., Coxe, S., Pelham, W. E., Rodriguez, L., Sanchez, F., Derefinko, K., Helseth, S., & Ward, A. (2016). Parent-teen behavior therapy + motivational interviewing for adolescents with ADHD. J Consult Clin Psychol, 84(8), 699-712. https://doi.org/10.1037/ccp0000106

180. Sibley, M. H., Pelham, W. E., Molina, B. S. G., Gnagy, E. M., Waschbusch, D. A., Garefino, A. C., Kuriyan, A. B., Babinski, D. E., & Karch, K. M. (2012). Diagnosing ADHD in adolescence. J Consult Clin Psychol, 80(1), 139-150. https://doi.org/10.1037/a0026577

181. Simpson, D., & Plosker, G. L. (2004). Atomoxetine: a review of its use in adults with attention deficit hyperactivity disorder. Drugs, 64(2), 205-222. https://doi.org/10.2165/00003495-200464020-00005

182. Sonuga-Barke, E. J., Daley, D., Thompson, M., Laver-Bradbury, C., & Weeks, A. (2001). Parent-based therapies for preschool attention-deficit/hyperactivity disorder: a randomized, controlled trial with a community sample. J Am Acad Child Adolesc Psychiatry, 40(4), 402-408. https://doi.org/10.1097/00004583-200104000-00008

183. Sonuga-Barke, E. J., Sergeant, J. A., Nigg, J., & Willcutt, E. (2008). Executive dysfunction and delay aversion in attention deficit hyperactivity disorder: nosologic and diagnostic implications. Child Adolesc Psychiatr Clin N Am, 17(2), 367-384, ix. https://doi.org/10.1016/j.chc.2007.11.008

184. Sourander, A., Sucksdorff, M., Chudal, R., Surcel, H. M., Hinkka-Yli-Salomäki, S., Gyllenberg, D., Cheslack-Postava, K., & Brown, A. S. (2019). Prenatal Cotinine Levels and ADHD Among Offspring. Pediatrics, 143(3). https://doi.org/10.1542/peds.2018-3144

185. Spencer, T., Biederman, J., Heiligenstein, J., Wilens, T., Faries, D., Prince, J., Faraone, S. V., Rea, J., Witcher, J., & Zervas, S. (2001). An open-label, dose-ranging study of atomoxetine in children with attention deficit hyperactivity disorder. J Child Adolesc Psychopharmacol, 11(3), 251-265. https://doi.org/10.1089/10445460152595577

186. Spencer, T., Biederman, J., Wilens, T., Prince, J., Hatch, M., Jones, J., Harding, M., Faraone, S. V., & Seidman, L. (1998). Effectiveness and tolerability of tomoxetine in adults with attention deficit hyperactivity disorder. Am J Psychiatry, 155(5), 693-695. https://doi.org/10.1176/ajp.155.5.693

187. Spetie, L., & Arnold, E. L. (2018). Attention-Deficit Hyperactivity Disorder. In A. Martin, M. H. Bloch, & F. R. Volkmar (Eds.), Lewis's child and adolescent psychiatry : a comprehensive textbook (5th ed., pp. 364-387). Wolters Kluwer Health/Lippincott Williams & Wilkins.

188. Sprafkin, J., Volpe, R. J., Gadow, K. D., Nolan, E. E., & Kelly, K. (2002). A DSM-IV-referenced screening instrument for preschool children: the Early Childhood Inventory-4. J Am Acad Child Adolesc Psychiatry, 41(5),

604-612. https://doi.org/10.1097/00004583-200205000-00018

189. Stein, M. A., Waldman, I. D., Charney, E., Aryal, S., Sable, C., Gruber, R., & Newcorn, J. H. (2011). Dose effects and comparative effectiveness of extended release dexmethylphenidate and mixed amphetamine salts. J Child Adolesc Psychopharmacol, 21(6), 581-588. https://doi.org/10.1089/cap.2011.0018

190. Steingard, R., Stein, M. A., & Markowitz, J. S. (2022). Medications Used for ADHD. In M. Dulcan (Ed.), Dulcan's Textbook of Child and Adolescent Psychiatry (Third ed., pp. 695-729). American Psychiatric Association Publishing.

191. Steingard, R., Taskiran, S., Connor, D. F., Markowitz, J. S., & Stein, M. A. (2019). New Formulations of Stimulants: An Update for Clinicians. J Child Adolesc Psychopharmacol, 29(5), 324-339. https://doi.org/10.1089/cap.2019.0043

192. Striley, C. W., Kelso-Chichetto, N. E., & Cottler, L. B. (2017). Nonmedical Prescription Stimulant Use Among Girls 10-18 Years of Age: Associations With Other Risky Behavior. J Adolesc Health, 60(3), 328-332. https://doi.org/10.1016/j.jadohealth.2016.10.013

193. Stringaris, A., Baroni, A., Haimm, C., Brotman, M., Lowe, C. H., Myers, F., Rustgi, E., Wheeler, W., Kayser, R., Towbin, K., & Leibenluft, E. (2010). Pediatric bipolar disorder versus severe mood dysregulation: risk for manic episodes on follow-up. J Am Acad Child Adolesc Psychiatry, 49(4), 397-405.

194. Stuckelman, Z. D., Mulqueen, J. M., Ferracioli-Oda, E., Cohen, S. C., Coughlin, C. G., Leckman, J. F., & Bloch, M. H. (2017). Risk of Irritability With Psychostimulant

Treatment in Children With ADHD: A Meta-Analysis. J Clin Psychiatry, 78(6), e648-e655. https://doi.org/10.4088/JCP.15r10601

195. Swanson, J. M., Arnold, L. E., Molina, B. S. G., Sibley, M. H., Hechtman, L. T., Hinshaw, S. P., Abikoff, H. B., Stehli, A., Owens, E. B., Mitchell, J. T., Nichols, Q., Howard, A., Greenhill, L. L., Hoza, B., Newcorn, J. H., Jensen, P. S., Vitiello, B., Wigal, T., Epstein, J. N., . . . Kraemer, H. C. (2017). Young adult outcomes in the follow-up of the multimodal treatment study of attention-deficit/hyperactivity disorder: symptom persistence, source discrepancy, and height suppression. J Child Psychol Psychiatry, 58(6), 663-678. https://doi.org/10.1111/jcpp.12684

196. Tannock, R. (2002). Cognitive correlates of ADHD. In P. S. Jesen, J. R. Cooper, & N. J. Kingston (Eds.), Attention Deficit Hyperactivity Disorder: State of the Science, Best Practices (pp. 818-827). Civic Research Institute.

197. Teitelman, E. (2001). Off-label uses of modafinil. Am J Psychiatry, 158(8), 1341. https://doi.org/10.1176/ajp.158.8.1341

198. Thapar, A., & Cooper, M. (2016). Attention deficit hyperactivity disorder. Lancet, 387(10024), 1240-1250. https://doi.org/10.1016/s0140-6736(15)00238-x

199. Thapar, A., Cooper, M., Eyre, O., & Langley, K. (2013). What have we learnt about the causes of ADHD? J Child Psychol Psychiatry, 54(1), 3-16. https://doi.org/10.1111/j.1469-7610.2012.02611.x

200. Thapar, A., Rice, F., Hay, D., Boivin, J., Langley, K., van den Bree, M., Rutter, M., & Harold, G. (2009). Prenatal smoking might not cause attention-deficit/hyperactivity disorder: evidence from a novel design. Biol Psychiatry,

66(8), 722-727.
https://doi.org/10.1016/j.biopsych.2009.05.032

201. Thurstone, C. (2019). Editorial: What Cures One Can Kill Another. J Am Acad Child Adolesc Psychiatry, 58(7), 661-662. https://doi.org/10.1016/j.jaac.2018.12.014

202. Tidy, H. L. (1938). Discussion on benzedrine: Uses and abuses. Proc R Soc Med, 32, 385-398.

203. Towbin, K., Vidal-Ribas, P., Brotman, M. A., Pickles, A., Miller, K. V., Kaiser, A., Vitale, A. D., Engel, C., Overman, G. P., Davis, M., Lee, B., McNeil, C., Wheeler, W., Yokum, C. H., Haring, C. T., Roule, A., Wambach, C. G., Sharif-Askary, B., Pine, D. S., . . . Stringaris, A. (2020). A Double-Blind Randomized Placebo-Controlled Trial of Citalopram Adjunctive to Stimulant Medication in Youth With Chronic Severe Irritability. J Am Acad Child Adolesc Psychiatry, 59(3), 350-361. https://doi.org/10.1016/j.jaac.2019.05.015

204. Tung, I., Li, J. J., Meza, J. I., Jezior, K. L., Kianmahd, J. S., Hentschel, P. G., O'Neil, P. M., & Lee, S. S. (2016). Patterns of Comorbidity Among Girls With ADHD: A Meta-analysis. Pediatrics, 138(4). https://doi.org/10.1542/peds.2016-0430

205. Vaishnavi, S., Gadde, K., Alamy, S., Zhang, W., Connor, K., & Davidson, J. R. (2006). Modafinil for atypical depression: effects of open-label and double-blind discontinuation treatment. J Clin Psychopharmacol, 26(4), 373-378. https://doi.org/10.1097/01.jcp.0000227700.263.75.39

206. van den Ban, E., Souverein, P., Meijer, W., van Engeland, H., Swaab, H., Egberts, T., & Heerdink, E. (2014). Association between ADHD drug use and injuries among

children and adolescents. Eur Child Adolesc Psychiatry, 23(2), 95-102. https://doi.org/10.1007/s00787-013-0432-8

207. Visser, J. C., Rommelse, N. N., Greven, C. U., & Buitelaar, J. K. (2016). Autism spectrum disorder and attention-deficit/hyperactivity disorder in early childhood: A review of unique and shared characteristics and developmental antecedents. Neurosci Biobehav Rev, 65, 229-263. https://doi.org/10.1016/j.neubiorev.2016.03.019

208. Visser, S. N., Blumberg, S. J., Danielson, M. L., Bitsko, R. H., & Kogan, M. D. (2013). State-based and demographic variation in parent-reported medication rates for attention-deficit/hyperactivity disorder, 2007-2008. Prev Chronic Dis, 10, E09. https://doi.org/10.5888/pcd9.120073

209. Volkow, N. D., Fowler, J. S., Logan, J., Alexoff, D., Zhu, W., Telang, F., Wang, G. J., Jayne, M., Hooker, J. M., Wong, C., Hubbard, B., Carter, P., Warner, D., King, P., Shea, C., Xu, Y., Muench, L., & Apelskog-Torres, K. (2009). Effects of modafinil on dopamine and dopamine transporters in the male human brain: clinical implications. Jama, 301(11), 1148-1154. https://doi.org/10.1001/jama.2009.351

210. Volkow, N. D., & Li, T. K. (2004). Drug addiction: the neurobiology of behaviour gone awry. Nat Rev Neurosci, 5(12), 963-970. https://doi.org/10.1038/nrn1539

211. Vrecko, S. (2013). Just How Cognitive Is "Cognitive Enhancement"? On the Significance of Emotions in University Students' Experiences with Study Drugs. AJOB Neurosci, 4(1), 4-12. https://doi.org/10.1080/21507740.2012.740141

212. Weiss, B. (1998). A risk assessment perspective on the neurobehavioral toxicity of endocrine disruptors. Toxicol

Ind Health, 14(1-2), 341-359.
https://doi.org/10.1177/074823379801400122

213. Wolraich, M. L., Hagan, J. F., Jr., Allan, C., Chan, E.,
Davison, D., Earls, M., Evans, S. W., Flinn, S. K.,
Froehlich, T., Frost, J., Holbrook, J. R., Lehmann, C. U.,
Lessin, H. R., Okechukwu, K., Pierce, K. L., Winner, J.
D., & Zurhellen, W. (2019). Clinical Practice Guideline
for the Diagnosis, Evaluation, and Treatment of Attention-
Deficit/Hyperactivity Disorder in Children and
Adolescents. Pediatrics, 144(4).
https://doi.org/10.1542/peds.2019-2528

214. Wolraich, M. L., Wilson, D. B., & White, J. W. (1995).
The effect of sugar on behavior or cognition in children. A
meta-analysis. Jama, 274(20), 1617-1621.
https://doi.org/10.1001/jama.1995.03530200053037

215. Xu, G., Strathearn, L., Liu, B., Yang, B., & Bao, W.
(2018). Twenty-Year Trends in Diagnosed Attention-
Deficit/Hyperactivity Disorder Among US Children and
Adolescents, 1997-2016. JAMA Netw Open, 1(4),
e181471.
https://doi.org/10.1001/jamanetworkopen.2018.1471

216. Yolton, K., Cornelius, M., Ornoy, A., McGough, J.,
Makris, S., & Schantz, S. (2014). Exposure to
neurotoxicants and the development of attention deficit
hyperactivity disorder and its related behaviors in
childhood. Neurotoxicol Teratol, 44, 30-45.
https://doi.org/10.1016/j.ntt.2014.05.003

217. Zetterqvist, J., Asherson, P., Halldner, L., Langstrom, N.,
& Larsson, H. (2013). Stimulant and non-stimulant
attention deficit/hyperactivity disorder drug use: total
population study of trends and discontinuation patterns
2006-2009. Acta Psychiatr Scand, 128(1), 70-77.
https://doi.org/10.1111/acps.12004

218. Zifko, U. A., Rupp, M., Schwarz, S., Zipko, H. T., & Maida, E. M. (2002). Modafinil in treatment of fatigue in multiple sclerosis. Results of an open-label study. J Neurol, 249(8), 983-987. https://doi.org/10.1007/s00415-002-0765-6

5

Some Preliminary Concepts for Prescribing Stimulants

(William Yvorchuk, MD CM)

As we pursue our study of the ramifications of stimulants for therapeutic purposes as well as the inevitable potential side effects and consequences of misuse and abuse, we should consider some general concepts about our neurobiology, particularly as it relates to our study of the consequences of Addiction also known as Substance Use Disorders (SUDs).

Some Basic Concepts in Neurobiology:

We should first begin our discussion with some background information regarding the brain pathways involved in Addiction which also pertain to the fundamental processes in our ongoing evaluation of the world around us. We constantly base our judgments on a foundation of expectation in any given situation and then compare the outcome in light of our current expectation.

Our inherent bias is to assess the outcome of any particular behavior on an emotional level. If anyone asked us out of the blue "How do we assess the world around us?" many would conclude that we are logical in our assessment of the various conditions that face us on a day-to-day basis.

We should however realize that we are far more emotional in our assessments than logical. We tend to assess the outcome of any given condition primarily on the basis of *reward* framed against the context of our expectation in the given situation. We inherently determine, at a *preconscious* level (before it arises in our level of conscious awareness), if the outcome meets our expectations, falls short of expectations, or surpasses our expectations.

This pattern of assessment occurs automatically, naturally, preconsciously and without forethought. The outcome simply presents itself to us and we then automatically form an evaluation on an emotional level which is processed through the mesolimbic-cortical (reward, dopaminergic) pathways. These pathways arise in the midbrain and connect with the higher cortex, the so-called gray matter of the brain. Our awareness of the outcome is processed in, and arises from, the frontal lobe of the brain, our forebrain region. This is generally the region where we determine our sense of self, the 'me', our innate experience of 'self-identification' and is thought to be the site of executive functioning and decision-making.

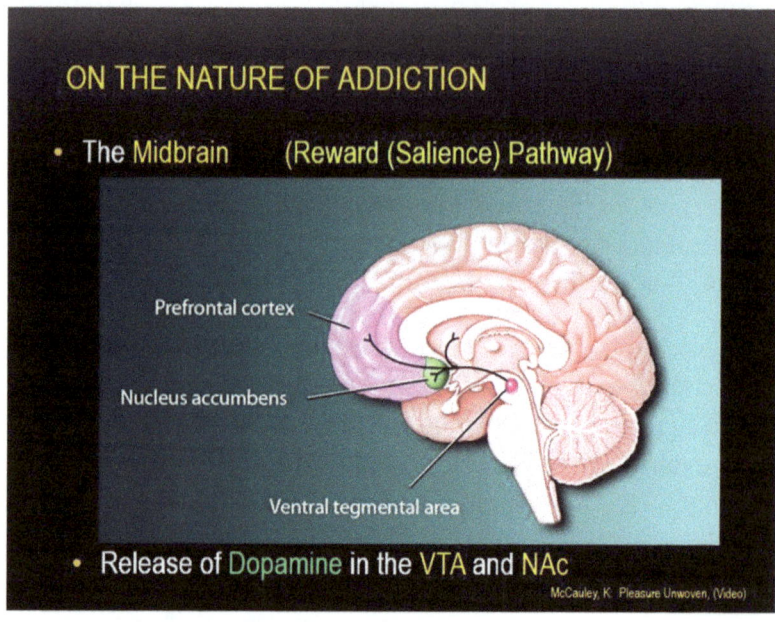

(Fig. 01 Adapted from McCauley K. *Pleasure Unwoven* (Video))

The generally accepted brain regions involved in our emotional assessment of outcomes are presented above. These are the so-called *dopamine* pathways involved in the development of the addictive behavioral response as well have a major influence on the development of our preconscious conditioning in our ongoing process of evaluating the world around us.

This is the same amalgam of pathways that determine our response to chronic pain (over 3 months in duration), where in fact the *magnitude of the perceived pain* is determined by an *emotional* center in the prefrontal cortex (PFC) (**1**).

A multitude of higher brain (cortical) regions within the gray matter send messages downward to converge on a region of the midbrain called the ventral tegmental area (VTA). The information is consolidated in this VTA region and the outcome leads to a response within the dopamine channel leading to a region called the nucleus accumbens (NAc) as well as directly to the prefrontal cortex (PFC) region. The NAc then sends messages, again through dopamine channels, to the anterior cingular cortex (ACC) and to the PFC. The net outcome of these transmissions is an automatic emotional assessment of whether we appreciate the experience or whether it falls short of expectations.

A simplified example may shed light on the discussion.

Let us assume that we face a bank of some 20 to 30 gumball machines. The premise presented to us is if we insert a quarter (25 cents), then we should receive two gumballs.

We approach one machine at random and insert the requisite quarter. We receive 2 gumballs in return as expected. The amount of dopamine released through the pathway is in keeping with the *expected* outcome. We then automatically take note of the result.

If, however, we approach another gumball machine, insert the quarter and receive only one gumball or none, the amount of dopamine is significantly reduced, thus informing us, on an *emotional* level, that the outcome was *not as expected*. We are disappointed and record the color, position and general characteristics of the disappointing machine so as to not return to it in the future.

We continue testing various machines with the usual return of two gumballs with an occasional one or none are produced.

If we then approach yet another machine, insert the quarter, turn the crank and in this case multiple gumballs fill our hand, the result of using this particular machine is *greater than expected*. A relative surplus of dopamine flows through the reward pathways. We are pleasantly surprised with the outcome and naturally pay attention to the various characteristics of the machine so if needed we can return straight to this one particular machine.

An *unexpectedly favorable* outcome generates a relative surplus of dopamine through the neural pathways and we are emotionally uplifted. Our cortex then sends an elevated series of transmissions back through the brain (glutamatergic pathways - glutamate-mediated pathways) to enhance the memories generated by this unexpectedly pleasant outcome. We experience a change in our state of being and find ourselves emotionally pleased and rewarded.

Again, if we yet approach another machine, insert the quarter, turn the crank and in this case a multitude of gumballs fall out, enough to fill both hands and spillover to the floor. The result of using this particular machine is *far greater than expected* and a relative flood of dopamine flows through our meso-cortical limbic (reward) pathways. [WY1]We will then vividly remember the color, position, style, and various qualities of the machine so as to return to it at a later date if we need many more gumballs to share with friends and find ourselves short of quarters!

This *unexpectedly and supremely favorable* outcome generates a relative flood of dopamine through the pathways, and we are markedly emotionally aroused and uplifted. Our cortex then sends a markedly heightened series of transmissions back through the brain (glutamatergic pathways) to lock in the memories generated by this unusually advantageous outcome. We experience an even more substantial change in our state of being and find ourselves markedly aroused.

The last example more closely resembles the process involved in the development of a relatively 'supernormal' (higher than normal) level of dopamine through the system. An even higher response is possible through the use of exogenous psychoactive chemicals such as substances of abuse. Under these conditions, the higher-than-normal flow of dopamine through the synapses of the system tend to provide for a 'supernormal' level of learning on an emotional level with the exaggerated memories and sensory perceptions of the event.

This is why many authors and addiction service providers consider that the use of the drugs of abuse allow for a 'supraphysiologic' level of learning thus anchoring the experience deeply in our nervous system. These qualities are reinforced through the repetitive use of the patient's drug of choice. Such experiential anchoring can be further enhanced with ongoing use of the drug when the subject finds themselves in a particularly depressed, anguished, oppressed and markedly stressed state, one from which there is no expectation of complete correction from the emotional distress and yet their drug of choice at a higher dose provides the amount of euphoria sufficient to counter the agony and then anchor the experience even more deeply.

Of course, after repeated episodes of substance use over a substantial period of time (months to years), the addict then adapts more to higher and higher levels of drug to now bring them back to an emotional equilibrium. It is at this juncture that the subject requires the drug simply to maintain an emotional equilibrium.

Furthermore, in the context of the 'supernormal' flood of dopamine under the condition above with the gumball machine providing a great surplus of gumballs, a very similar condition could be experienced in a casino facing a bank of slot machines. The unexpected outcome of hitting a large jackpot would likely create the same effect on our nervous system. With the understanding that we know it will be unlikely that this particular machine will not return another jackpot anytime soon, many would surmise that they now feel 'lucky' and would then keep playing the slots and return on other days to play the slots again and again for yet more emotional stimulation hoping for another *great reward*.

These simplistic examples can be elaborated in complexity to present various conditions we face on a day-to-day basis with similar nuanced results. We typically judge events through an emotional lens whether we are consciously aware of it or not. We are primarily emotional beings rather than strictly 'logical' ones.

The last of the four examples presented above is also similar to that which is experienced when our nervous system is markedly aroused through a supra-physiologic response when we find ourselves in a debilitating emotional state and ingest a favorable controlled substance, a drug of choice, as we discussed somewhat earlier. Another suitable example would be to find ourselves in a marked state of agitated anxiety and then taking a substantial dose of a potent fast-acting benzodiazepine such as alprazolam. A typical effect produced would be to suddenly shift our emotional state from marked anxiety to one completely devoid of anxiety. The expectation of improvement would be vastly superseded. Such a dramatic emotional shift could lead one to crave the response afforded by this potent benzodiazepine again and again.

Similar conditions could arise in certain prone individuals after the ingestion of particular opiates such as oxycodone, hydrocodone, morphine, hydromorphone, fentanyl or diacetylmorphine (heroin), or sufficient amounts of alcohol.

The arousal of exaggerated physiologic responses to controlled substances, as compared to the apparent and muted effects from naturalistic practices such as stress management, breathing exercises, meditation and mindfulness, promote the demand for rapid resolution of emotional dis-ease through pharmacologic interventions despite the plethora of potential side effects, particularly as dosages rise.

Another example of the influence of the mesolimbic cortical system on our overall emotional state, but in the direction of the reversal of reward (anti-reward), could be presented under the conditions of protracted stress that tend to mute the dopamine response through negative feedback loops and under which we experience a lack of pleasurable responses.

If the conditions persist for a sufficient period of time, we may be led to a condition termed anhedonia, which refers to the condition in which we experience little to no pleasure. Freedom from the experience of stress and its oppressive weight then becomes our prime motivating factor.

Under prolonged conditions of emotional suppression it is not uncommon to be exposed to a substance with substantial emotional potency such as alcohol, sedatives such as benzodiazepines (e.g. alprazolam, lorazepam, diazepam, clonazepam), opioids (e.g. morphine, heroin, hydrocodone, hydromorphone, oxycodone, fentanyl), stimulants (e.g. methylphenidate, amphetamine salts, methamphetamine, cocaine, 'crack' cocaine, 'bath salts', 'Ecstasy', 'Molly'), marijuana, hallucinogens (e.g. LSD, mescaline, psilocybin, ayahuasca) and dissociative agents (e.g. ketamine, PCP), or inhalational agents (e.g. nitrous oxide ('laughing gas'), 'Poppers', various solvents, aerosol sprays and gases). We may then become prone to demanding the sudden and pervasive emotional correction of our state of distress through pharmacologic means. A process of immediate gratification. Our nervous system can become functionally 'hijacked' by the 'key' chemical that most fits the 'lock' of our nervous system. Our demand for immediate gratification no longer needs to await the favorable response from the effects of more prolonged holistic, stress relief practices.

A particular substance can be thought of as the 'key to the lock' of our particular nervous system and when ingested we typically undergo an unusually large emotional shift leading to supra-physiologic shifts in dopamine neurotransmitter under the influence of the substance. It is not uncommon to then have an unusually large pleasurable response to stress relief that is not experienced *except* for under the circumstances of the substance use. The dopamine levels shoot up markedly and we experience an unexpectedly satisfying emotional response. If we continue to use the substance for emotional modulation in effectively dispelling our usual burden of stress, we may then 'groove' a supra-physiologic dopamine response along with the *heightened* memories of the *substance use*. It would not be then much of an intellectual stretch to consider that after repeated use of such effective emotionally modulating chemicals, we could become emotionally 'dependent' on their use to shift our unpleasant emotional state. This effectively begins a behavioral path toward a substance use disorder (SUD) in relying on the effective emotional shift provided by our chemical substance of choice.

Our behavior rises to the level of addiction, or SUD, once we continue to ingest a substance, for the emotional relief, despite an accumulation of negative physical and/or life consequences. This scenario of essentially 'behavior out of control' despite consequences provides the hallmark of addictive chemical use (or behavioral addiction such as in gambling, gaming or internet use of various nature).

Universal Aspect of the Limbic System:

It is interesting to note at this juncture, that the field of addiction medicine and its treatment has relied on the laboratory development of models of addictive disease in mice and rat populations. Happily, these studies are not then replicated in higher mammalian forms such as cats, dogs, or primates. It is not necessary to replicate the studies in higher mammals before beginning to consider treatment in humans because *all mammals* have the same *subcortical* structures. The amount of gray matter, or cerebral cortex, differentiates mankind from other mammals, yet the subcortical structures are all present in all mammalian species.

The inference is that the range and condition of emotional responses in mammals are shared among all mammals. The fear response remains the same for all. Behavior consistent with empathy and compassion have been observed in other mammalian species. It would be favorable to retain these considerations in mind as we interface with nature.

The difference between mankind and the mammalian animal kingdom is our development of self-identification from which the other mammalian species are exempt. Self-reflective consciousness and self-referential processing do not occur in other mammals. The constant stream of consciousness we refer to as the mind does not plague nature. There is no malice to be found in nature. Nor is there any sense of victimhood or self-pity which remains the foundational experience of human addictive behavior.

All of the subcortical structures are evident in all mammalian species. A behavioral model of addiction has even been developed in mice and rat strains.

The proposed solutions for the problem of addiction in mankind are tested in rats and mice populations and then extrapolated directly to testing at the human level.

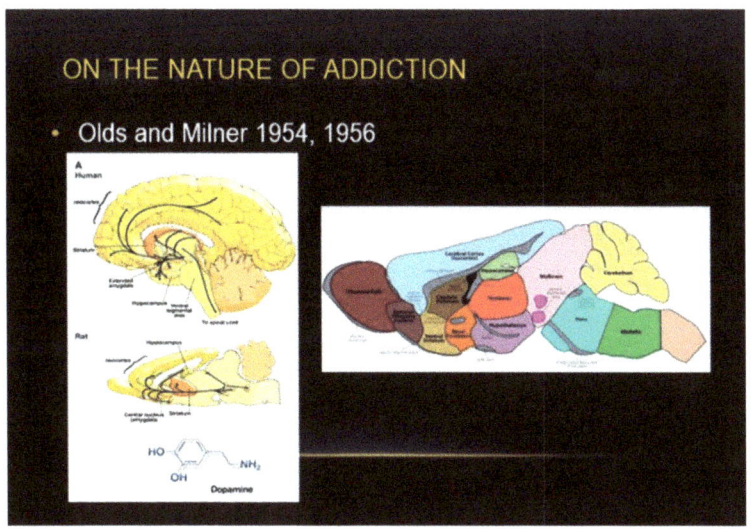

(Fig. 02 Adapted from Olds and Milner)

(Olds J, Milner P. Positive reinforcement produced by electrical stimulation of the septal area and other regions of rat brain. *J Comp Physiol Psychol*. 1954;47:419-27)

(Olds J. Pleasure centers in the brain. *Sci Am*. 1956;195:105-16)

As we can see in the images above, the cortex of humans is more elaborate than that of a rat but we "share the same subcortical structures" (statement from Eliot Gardner, PhD; Chief, Neuropsychopharmacology Section, Intramural Research Program, NIDA and NIH; ASAM Board Review Course 2012 (Lecture - Neurobiology of Addiction; 20220920-22)).

All of the brain components underlying the cortical structures (gray matter) of the brain are present and similar in all mammalian species. This provides for some pertinent insight when we consider such activities as hunting for sport and the treatment of animals in slaughterhouses and the dairy industry. Notwithstanding our treatment of other creatures, the field of addiction medicine has provided for substantial insights into our emotional underpinnings as well as the path of recovery we all share.

Recovery from addiction is primarily an emotional recovery rather than a behavioral one. The core premise is to undergo a shift in emotional experience such that we then no longer require the chemical substances as a solution to our emotional condition. As we will explore later in this manuscript, the prime condition that is altered so as to allow for an actual cure from addiction arises from the experience of a shift in perceived identity. We forego the experience of all self-pity in surrendering our core perception of victimhood.

A Personal Perspective on the Core Experiential Problem in Addiction:

Although most of the information presented on the topic of Addiction in this manuscript is drawn from a body of broadly accepted work in the field, it seems appropriate at present to provide an element of originality and uniqueness. The reason this perspective is presented lies in a fundamental weakness in the disease model for mental health conditions.

We have a remarkable appreciation for the disease elements of substance use disorders. Our body of knowledge is growing every year as new information emerges with respect to neurobiology, neurotransmitter systems, pathways in the brain, feedback loops, etc., but we pay little attention to the ongoing *experience* of addiction and its recovery. Neurotransmitter systems cannot be addressed through our level of awareness. Our internal experience of consciousness does not allow us to modulate recovery from an emotional condition, or addiction, through the active engagement of pathways at the exclusion of others.

Our internal emotional environment arises to our conscious awareness from a vast morass of subconscious (preconscious) processes. This leads to a disjunction between what is processed at the pre-cortical level and our conscious experience thereof. Carl Jung referred to the experience as reflective of our 'shadow' selves, the broad, pre-perceptual complex of our conditioning. We are affected emotionally by a host of former experiences beginning in early childhood. We seldom remain aware of all of the influences that have come to play in our emotional development over our lifetime. We often bury a multitude of memories and experiences, particularly if they are too painful to recall. These experiences nonetheless profoundly shape the nature of our internal, pre-conscious environment. These experiential memories of failed expectation are processed through dopaminergic pathways discussed above. It is not unusual to discover that a patient with a SUD has suffered some form of repressed childhood trauma. It is felt that a majority of patients suffering from addiction have experienced childhood trauma.

We are in touch with an internal *experience* of our cumulative emotional conditioning. The result of all of these preconscious processes arises as our immediate emotional state and the conscious mind-stream of thought to which we are exposed on a moment-to-moment basis. Our experience of the mind is the product of our preconscious processes. It is an 'afterimage' of subconscious processing. The overall present-moment experience is strongly tied to our experience of our 'selves'. The composite 'me' derives from an amalgam of a lifetime of emotionally laden events. We will come to appreciate in the pages that follow, as we discuss the nature of addiction on the background of ADD/ADHD, that effective recovery from a substance use disorder arises from a renewed experience of 'me', particularly one that has been released from the prolonged conditioning of victimization and self-pity.

A Seminal Question with a Surprising Result:

The perspective we address at this juncture was cultivated over a number of years in the field of addiction medicine as a medical provider to patients with substance use disorder. Conservatively, some 400 to 500 consecutive addiction patients over a period of 5 to 7 years in a single provider practice were asked whether they could identify with the following scenario.

The unexpected outcome was that virtually 100% of patients agree with the elements of the experience described regardless of their gender, age, the nature of their substance of choice, or whether or not they were subject to childhood trauma. It is unusual to say the least that one could project 100% agreement with any particular scenario, but the elements described below seem to undergird a common experience of substance use in such a fashion that it supports a lack of behavioral control despite negative consequences, the very definition of a substance use disorder (addiction).

As we read the proposed experience under the influence of the patient's drug of choice, we should firmly keep in mind that the references to the emotional ties to the past and to the future reflect the perception of victimization with an underlying foundation in self-pity, whether it presents to the subject at the conscious level or remains suppressed from conscious awareness at the repressed, preconscious level.

When one has a positive experience with the drug of choice, is the experience consistent with the following scenario?

Over the entire course of our lives, we take in, we absorb, emotional information (the experiential movement is from outward to inward) and we tend to push this emotional distress downward, and store it in our 'basement' so to speak. However, for some of us the emotional tension fills our 'basement' and periodically, we begin to feel a profound emotional distress rise from deep within. We feel deeply uncomfortable in our skin and seek immediate emotional relief from this pervasive sense of suffering.

We begin to feel like a 'pressure cooker' as the emotional tension builds inside; our minds are busy and incessantly spinning, oftentimes out of control; we feel oppressed within and without; the world seems to bear down on us; and we feel as though we will cave into ourselves despite the profound emotional distress bubbling forth. We desperately seek some form of relief, but we haven't learned how to effectively release the emotional distress experientially.

As a result, because we have been conditioned to 'take in' information, either we find it (our drug of choice) or it finds us. We nonetheless have learned to ingest (take in) a mood-altering substance so as to effectively and immediately relieve this profound emotional tension, and three things seem to happen as we are relieved of this profound emotional disturbance.

(1) Our emotional hardship (... guilt, shame, remorse, anguish, resentment, anger, fury, ...) is pushed away into the past and seems to move out of the reach of our immediate experience

Our fear for the future (...anxiety, catastrophizing, fear of consequences of using the chemical(s), life and loss, ...) is pushed away and also moves beyond our immediate experiential grasp

We then feel as though time has slipped away as we are freed from the emotional distress, and we then move much more deeply into a 'present moment' experience. The past is pushed away and the future as well. We are then left with 'Here and Now' which is much more comfortable.

(2) The mind that was formerly so incessantly busy has now calmed down considerably and has moved us toward the experience of a 'quiet mind'.

(3) Furthermore, we have finally moved toward the experience of having been 'freed from our 'selves' (ego; compounded emotional burden; conditioning) and because this 'me' is so tightly bound to the world, the world as well seems to have moved some distance away and has provided us with some solace and emotional peace.

A 'space' free from ourselves has now opened for us in which to dwell for a time in an emotionally deeply peaceful place.

The 3 consequences that arise from using our drug of choice become:

(1) A movement toward the experience of a substantially 'quieter mind';

(2) at some distance from the experience of time, thus moving us toward the experience of the 'right here and right now';

(3) along with a sense of 'freedom from ourselves' and thus some 'freedom from the world' in general.

The overall experiential movement under the chemical influence is rapid and substantial, moving us toward (but not extending to) the experience of:

No 'me'; No mind; No time

(A reduction in the experience of time automatically decreases the experience of suffering in relation to the past (depression) and to that of the future (anxiety))

The patient is then asked if this is consistent with their experience under the influence of their chemical of choice and the answer has been uniformly in the affirmative.

The following question then arises - why is this the case?

*The answer lies in the accurate assessment of our **true emotional baseline**.*

Most of us believe that our emotional baseline lies in having a comfortable and functional 'ego' in this hectic world, yet this may not be the case. Our life experience begins in a profoundly stable, baseline emotional state once we are first brought into the world.

If we can only imagine being a complete 'stranger in a strange land' as we all were as newborns. We did not know anything of this world. We were complete and absolute strangers to it. We had no preconceived thoughts, ideas, concepts or beliefs. We did not know what a human being was nor anything else in the world for that matter. We had no concept of mother, father, or family. Furthermore, we were completely powerless and at the absolute mercy of our caregiver(s). Everyone was a stranger, and we could not do anything for ourselves. We could not clean ourselves; could not feed ourselves; could not protect ourselves; and had no control whatsoever over our environment; nor could we communicate any experience of dis-ease if we felt anything wrong. We were functionally 'locked in'. If this were a mature (ego-centric) adult suddenly exposed to these unusual circumstances, they would be in major distress and could barely cope with the situation for any length of time. Yet newborns are at perfect peace.

This experiential state of blissful peace despite a complete apparent alienation from the world is our actual emotional baseline. It provides for a profound sense of peace ('the peace that surpasses understanding') regardless of the environmental circumstances.

This 'peace that surpasses understanding' arises from our original experiential state, which can most simply be described as:

No 'me' - No mind - No time.

*As we all begin this life's journey with the experience beyond 'self' and thus beyond thought, there is no sense of time. We only experience the **present moment** without any experience of self (me) or time.*

This is a universal experience regardless of our heredity or heritage; regardless of nature or nurture. Every one of us born into this world comes into it with the same underlying experience of - 'no me (self), no mind, no time'.

One reason that drugs of abuse are so difficult to forego is that they become the chemical 'key to the lock' of our emotional nervous system. They become the most efficient and rapid means to experientially shift us from the emotional distress experienced within ourselves to that freedom from ourselves and toward our *universal baseline* state of *experiential peace*. These chemicals provide for a *supra-physiologic* release of neurotransmitters that cannot be easily duplicated experientially through naturalistic methods.

The next observation that arises is: if we can move toward this universal baseline state of emotional freedom from self with a profoundly quiet mind and thus with a vast reduction in the sense of time without the use of substances of abuse, then we should not need them for our emotional recovery. A simple observation is that in the vast majority of circumstances 'everything is fine right here and right now'. If we can be freed from our underlying, stored, emotional baggage, our emotional conditioning, then we are at a much greater advantage to be released from emotional dependence on drugs of abuse. The critical factor is that we need to walk a path of (emotional) recovery with the intent of developing a renewed experience of our identity. One that is dramatically reduced in the perception of victimization so as to reduce and ablate all experience of resentment.

The surprising observation, identified once we find ourselves in complete and stable recovery, is that we experience a radically new and muted (subdued) identity. It is our identification in and with victimization, along with the resultant ongoing experience of resentment and self-pity, that chains us to addiction and our preferred substance of abuse. The change in identity begets a renewed experience of the world in general and with everyone and everything in it.

This perspective presents a fairly radical departure from traditional modes of addiction treatment such as cognitive behavioral therapy (CBT), behavior modification (BM), 12 Step work, SMART recovery practice, or even Celebrate Recovery and therapeutic community (TC) systems. The practice of surrendering victimization dovetails seamlessly with the recovery practices described above and with the daily holistic practices of sleep hygiene, stress management, meditation and mindfulness. All methods mentioned above can be practiced in concert to direct us toward the ongoing experience of surrendering our attachment to victimhood and suffering, along with a perpetual state of forgiveness for everyone and everything that has happened to us in the past, and with a focus to experience life in a present-moment awareness of 'right here and right now'. The focus of attention should eventually be on our actual moment to moment experience of life rather than the perpetual state of attention to the mind as a lens through which we perceive everything around us.

The approach espoused above depends on our fundamental common ground of emotional experience, and is essentially measured as a function of *perceived identity*. The path becomes one of surrender of attachment to victimhood and self-pity through a core practice of ultimately forgiving everyone for everything that we have ever been endured in our past. We must ultimately let go of all attachment to victimhood. Such a practice undermines the emotional structure and form of the conditioned 'self' and can lead to an effective subsidence of the perceived 'me'. Insofar that we relinquish attachment to self-pity and suffering, we move in the direction of profound emotional healing with a vastly reduced reliance on exogenous chemicals for abrupt emotional modulation.

The experience of a shift in perceived identity is in essence the same shift that occurs for many addicted women who suddenly relinquish their substance of abuse once they discover they have become pregnant. By no means does every woman who becomes pregnant release attachment to their drug of choice, but many do. When asked how they were able to accomplish this outcome, many do not actually know, or merely report a change as a result of their knowledge of their pregnant state and the child they bear within.

If we focus on this *shift in perception*, we come to the universal answer to the emotional strife that we all harbor within. Namely, our experience of life can change dramatically once a modicum of selflessness, or innocence, is perceived within our being. A 'new mother' experiences a shift within that accommodates the inclusion of another *innocent* being. The incorporation of an element of innocence and selflessness within the perceived self can precipitate a surrender of the ingestion of substances potentially harmful to the fetus. The mother's addiction is effectively mitigated, albeit temporarily.

After delivery, some mothers do not return to their substance use. Some return to their substance use disorder in a muted fashion, while others return to their full-blown addiction evident prior to pregnancy. The essential element for change lies in the nature of their underlying perceived identification. Those who return to their former experience of self, regardless of the presence of a newborn in their lives, return to former use. Those who adopt an element of selflessness on behalf of their child tend not to return completely to their former 'selves' and pathologic behavior.

Keeping this perspective in mind as we navigate the following pages may well add insight into the underpinnings of substance use disorders and assist in consolidating a practical approach to the treatment of addiction.

References:

1.Baliki MN, et al. Chronic Pain and the Emotional Brain: Specific Brain Activity Associated with Spontaneous Fluctuations of Intensity of Chronic Back Pain

Journal of Neuroscience, November 22, 2006 • 26(47):12165-12173.

ADHD and Risk of Addiction

(William Yvorchuk, MD CM)

Cause of Attention-Deficit / Hyperactivity Disorder:

The exact causes of ADHD are not yet fully known with certainty. ADHD is felt to arise from issues related to the DAT (dopamine transporter gene) and the D4 dopamine receptor (DRD4) **(1)(2)(3)(4)(5)**. It has been suggested that certain abnormalities in the dopamine transporter genes are associated with ADHD as well as substance use disorders (SUDs)**(6)(7)(8)**.

The subsequent behavioral issues relate to abnormalities in *executive functioning* where children with ADHD have aberrancies in the development of certain regions of the brain as compared to children without the condition. The condition can extend through childhood and adolescence and continue into adulthood. Adults who have ADHD universally had the disorder in childhood and retain a functionally 'sluggish' dopamine transmission system.

The end result is that there is a problem in dopamine transmission along dopaminergic pathways that lead to problems in message transmission and also result in a lower degree of gray matter development in areas linked to these dopaminergic pathways. Improvement in transmission across synaptic clefts and thus in transmission along particular nerve pathways arises from the use of exogenous agents, such as amphetamines, which increase the effective amount of dopamine in the synaptic cleft.

An effective analogy is akin to the upstream neurons along the pathway are overworked and running as fast as they can to provide the requisite amount of dopamine across the synapse. Due to problems with the receptor or the transporter gene, a functionally insufficient amount of dopamine activity ensues in the terminal of the post-synaptic (downstream) neuron.

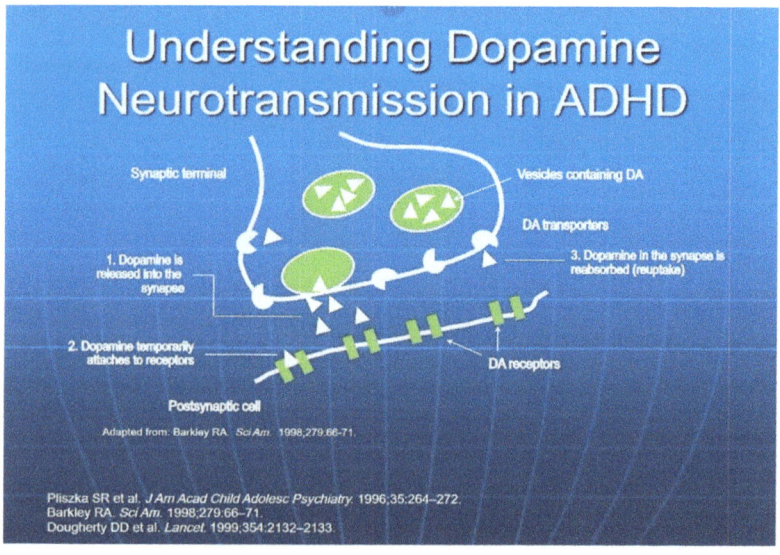

(Fig 01. Adapted from lecture by (Daniel Kelleher MD (Tri State Neuro-Psych Inc) ADD)
(https://slideplayer.com/slide/2366686/)
(Image in turn Adapted from)

(Barkley RA. Attention-deficit hyperactivity disorder. Sci Am. 1998 Sep;279(3):66-71) (doi: 10.1038/scientificamerican0998-66. PMID: 9725940)

The upstream neurons in the involved higher cortical centers are 'running as fast as they can' yet the downstream neurons experience a functionally insufficient amount of excitation for efficient function and the overall system misfunctions. The higher cortical brain is working excessively and the lower centers remain insufficient thus giving rise to and possibly exaggerating the functional symptoms of ADHD with a predominance on either hyperactivity, impulsiveness, distractedness and lack of restraint, attention and focus depending on the specific pathways affected to a greater or lesser degree in the individual.

Under these conditions, when the patient ingests a medication or substance that allows for a greater degree of dopamine release in the synaptic cleft then more is made available to provide for transmission of an impulse in the following neuron. The synapse seemingly becomes more efficient, and the pathway is restored back toward normalization with the upstream (higher cortex) neurons quieting down because they do not have to work as hard in providing for dopamine transmission across the synapse. Further, the downstream neurons are sufficiently excited to function in normalized fashion and the feedback loop normalizes.

This appears on the surface of overall behavior in the individual as a paradoxical reaction (response) to the ingestion of (e.g.) amphetamines or cocaine. The overall effect of ingesting these potent stimulants is not to provide for stimulation of the individual rather it functionally normalizes behavior. In this sense, the paradoxical response to stimulants is a normalization of the internal experience which becomes a normalization of external behavior. Furthermore, this seemingly paradoxical response appears to be protective for addiction and substance abuse in the patient with *true* ADHD.

In the context of addiction, during parties where cocaine might be freely available and consumed to provide for energy to keep partying all night, the functional outlier is the person who ingests cocaine and then seems to quiet down and possibly even go to sleep on the couch during the party. This person's brain functionally quieted down under the influence of the potent stimulant, and they relaxed or even felt too tired to stay awake. This individual is a person with *true* ADHD.

Under these conditions, the stimulant provides for a paradoxical response which appears to be protective for the individual because of a normalization of their neurophysiology rather than the functional arousal or euphoria engendered in others who experience paradoxical reactions to various substances of abuse.

Paradoxical responses to some substances of abuse:

We may at this juncture consider various responses to classic substances of abuse and the posited experience underlying the addiction if it develops in a particular individual.

We will limit ourselves to the consideration of specific facets that come into play in the various substance use disorders merely to illustrate the point that our internal experience is the factor that drives us to whether or not we will either be more or less likely to develop an addiction to a substance of abuse.

Alcohol Use Disorder:

In the situation of excessive use of alcohol, there are two general and overarching experiences that come into play. The first relates to the paradoxical response to alcohol in developing a euphoria after use. The second relates to the experiential escape from profound anxiety such as post-traumatic stress disorder (PTSD).

Under normal conditions, most people consume alcohol to provide for a change of state, an internal experience of freedom from our current internal emotional experience. In this sense the usual response is a rather gentle shift toward emotional release and freedom from our current experience of stress. The more we consume, the greater the response and the majority are satisfied with the shift in the internal emotional state after one or two standard-measured alcoholic beverages. This provides a certain amount of internal experiential release without the loss of control most individuals abhor. This level of use then provides for a limited shift in emotional experience. Hence, the National Institute on Alcohol Abuse and Alcoholism (NIAAA) apportioned standards for at-risk drinking (**9**).

NIAAA - Drinking Levels Defined (Standards for Alcohol Consumption):

Binge Drinking:

NIAAA defines binge drinking as a pattern of drinking alcohol that brings blood alcohol concentration (BAC) to 0.08 percent - or 0.08 grams of alcohol per deciliter - or higher. For a typical adult, this pattern corresponds to consuming 5 or more drinks (male), or 4 or more drinks (female), in about 2 hours.

The Substance Abuse and Mental Health Services Administration (**SAMHSA**), which conducts the annual National Survey on Drug Use and Health (NSDUH), defines binge drinking as 5 or more alcoholic drinks for males or 4 or more alcoholic drinks for females on the same occasion (i.e., at the same time or within a couple of hours of each other) on at least 1 day in the past month.

SAMHSA defines heavy alcohol use as binge drinking on 5 or more days in the past month.

Heavy Alcohol Use:

NIAAA defines heavy drinking as follows:

For men, consuming more than 4 drinks on any day or more than 14 drinks per week

For women, consuming more than 3 drinks on any day or more than 7 drinks per week

SAMHSA defines heavy alcohol use as binge drinking on 5 or more days in the past month.

Under conditions of alcohol use disorder (AUD), typically the amounts of ingestion presented above are exceeded. It is still possible to qualify for an AUD without exceeding the limits imposed above if the hallmark of the diagnosis of addiction is present, namely, ongoing behavior despite continued presence of negative consequences.

A certain individual may be prone to developing an AUD if they have a paradoxical reaction to the use of alcohol by developing a state of euphoria with alcohol ingestion (**10**)(**11**). Their response may or may not be somewhat exaggerated for the amount of alcohol ingested. The pertinent facet is not the suppression or abatement of an aroused emotional state as in a typical response to the ingestion of a sedative such as alcohol, a barbiturate, a benzodiazepine or an opiate. Rather, there arises a state of euphoria, possibly along with an increase in the level of energy perceived. Sedation may come later but the initial response is more of one of euphoria, a state of inordinate happiness, wellbeing and potentially excitement. The craving to escape oneself to experience the state of euphoria on a recurrent basis may lead an individual to excess alcohol consumption with all of the negative physical, as well as psychosocial, and behavioral consequences. This is the form of AUD that responds better to the use of Naltrexone, an opioid blocker, because it is felt that the state of euphoria may be endorphin-mediated. Naltrexone blocks the action of endorphins that mediate the state of euphoria with alcohol use. Naltrexone has been found to improve the condition of alcohol use disorder in relation to a reduction in drinking-days and the amount of alcohol consumed on any given drinking day (**12**).

Insofar that cravings for substance use in general are also thought to be endorphin-mediated, Naltrexone should also be helpful to reduce the craving for the relevant substance of dependence in a particular individual.

There is an alternate form of AUD. This form is primarily related to assuaging a pervasive and overwhelming state of chronic anxiety through the use of excess levels of alcohol. The individual ingests alcohol to alleviate the internal experience of severely functionally compromising anxiety such as in PTSD. These individuals typically drink to blackout. Subjects who drink to alleviate a chronic and pervasive state of anxiety are typically the 'nasty drunk' rather than the aforementioned euphoric and 'happy' drunk.

Patients who treat their profound anxiety with alcohol typically move through different experiential stages during a bout of alcohol consumption. They begin with the premise that they require an excess of alcohol to 'functionally' treat their profound, markedly elevated state of anxiety. The patient begins in a state that is essentially non-functional or very poorly functional from their extreme anxiety. They begin ingesting alcohol and as the chemical takes effect, they begin to experience a disinhibition (lack of emotional restraint) because the activity of the PFC dampening centers is reduced. This commonly gives rise to a functionally heightened state of misbehavior resulting from the underlying marked anxiety state. The angry drunk emerges. The individual typically drinks more because more alcohol is required to affect a dampening of the underlying anxiety state. It is not uncommon for the subject to finally reach the desired level of emotional dampening during the ongoing ingestion of excess alcohol, but it can often occur with a residual amount of alcohol still in the stomach and upper digestive track which has yet to be absorbed. The individual finally begins to feel more 'comfortable in their own skin', then the residual alcohol continues to be absorbed, and the blood alcohol (BAC) level then continues to rise. This delayed effect of a 'supernormal' BAC level often leads to the experience of blackout. This blackout can lead to a perceived improvement in sleep, resolution of insomnia, amnesia for the events occurring just before or during this functional cognitive 'blackout'. It is not uncommon for people to not remember how they got home or other events that may have transpired during the so-called blackout.

Alcohol use disorder can arise in either situation. Naltrexone is more efficient in the first scenario discussed. In either case, the individual is loath to refrain from alcohol use because they feel their very well-being, their emotional foundation, depends on the use of their substance of choice.

Acute alcohol withdrawal leads to marked anxiety and possibly even to life-threatening seizures or serious and potentially life-threatening cardiovascular events, such as myocardial infarction (MI), stroke (CVA) or rupture of an aneurysm. The delayed aspect of alcohol withdrawal, post-acute alcohol withdrawal (PAW), is experienced as a heightening of the underlying anxiety condition which then draws patients back into the cycle of excess alcohol use.

The issue to remember in our current context is that the paradoxical response to alcohol in providing for a state of euphoria can lead to an AUD.

The alternate condition is one of self-medication of a profound, pervasive, markedly elevated and functionally compromising state of anxiety.

Benzodiazepine Use Disorder:

In the situation of excessive use of sedatives such as benzodiazepines (or barbiturates), there are two general and overarching experiences that come into play as in the case of alcohol use disorder (AUD).

As in the excessive use of alcohol, the first relates to the paradoxical development of an initial state of euphoria with the use of benzodiazepines or barbiturates. Thus, similar conditions are in play as discussed above.

The second situation is again common with the profound and marked condition of anxiety assuaged by the intake of excess amounts of the preferred sedative as with the use of alcohol discussed above.

Potent benzodiazepines with a short half-life (quicker effect and dissipation), such as alprazolam, are more prone to abuse.

As we discussed, the same take home point is the potential for a sedative abuse condition deriving from the paradoxical response to the benzodiazepine or barbiturate.

Opioid / Opiate Use Disorder:

Although some patients feel a substantial improvement in anxiety under the influence of opiates, the development of an Opioid / Opiate Use Disorder (OUD) virtually *never* occurs *unless* the individual first experiences the paradoxical response of euphoria, or the arousal of energy, from the use of immediate-release opiates.

It is possible for a subject, who eventually develops an OUD condition, to begin taking opiates for an acute event such as an injury or surgery without experiencing the substantial 'lift' of energy from the opiate. It is only once an individual experiences or begins to experience a substantial euphoria or energy arousal that the risk of developing the OUD arises. What specifically gives rise to the 'switch' from the lack of the euphoric or energy response to one where it is present still remains in question.

It is however known to clinicians that it is this experience of a paradoxical response of euphoria or energy to the use of an immediate-release (IR) opiate that defines the potential to develop an OUD. In our practice, having treated hundreds of patients with OUD, not a single patient reported not 'getting energy' from IR opiates.

This paradoxical response to the use of opiates characterizes the evolution to the development of OUD.

The Situation with Stimulants:

As can be suspected, the situation with the effects of stimulants is the reverse of the development of a Substance Use Disorder (SUD) with sedatives.

Whereas the paradoxical effect from the use of sedatives (alcohol, benzodiazepines and opiates) enhances the experiential response to the drugs and raises the risk toward a Use Disorder, the paradoxical response in ADHD to the use of stimulants seems to provide a protective effect.

The natural response to the use of stimulants, in those without an underlying, pervasive and markedly elevated anxiety state, is an increase in energy, well-being, focus, productivity and possibly a full-blown euphoria.

This is the major problem faced by the clinician who treats patients with ADHD and their family members. The ADHD patient benefits physiologically from treatment with stimulants, but their close relatives or acquaintances, who do not have the condition and experiment with the substances, may also derive a *perceived* emotional, functional and experiential benefit from their use. They may even consider themselves as having ADHD because of the perceived resultant benefit to their daily functioning.

The most important distinction is therefore lost to the individual user. The 'normal' individual, who is not experiencing a paradoxical response to the potent stimulant, feels better emotionally and functionally with its use. However, they do *not* have any functional abnormalities *without* the use of the stimulant substances. Whereas, the *true* ADHD patient cannot function effectively without the stimulant.

There is a vast difference in response to controlled substance stimulants in the true ADHD patient as opposed to a 'normal' individual. The ADHD patient remains *objectively*, functionally compromised without the use of the stimulants. The individual who ingests stimulants but does not have ADHD falls prey to the *perceived* emotional and functional improvement. The latter is prone to a Stimulant Use Disorder (StiUD). The true ADHD patient is markedly less likely to develop the problem because their internal experience and external function returns toward normal. There is a relief from the use of the stimulant, not a rise in energy, focus, well-being or euphoria.

Medications Used to Treat True ADHD:

Medications such as methylphenidate (Ritalin®) and amphetamine salts (Adderall®) that block the DAT (dopamine transporter) thus improving activity at the level of the post-synaptic dopamine receptor improve symptoms of ADD/ADHD.

It is interesting to note that *amphetamine* is substantially *more* potent than *cocaine* in making dopamine (DA) available in the synaptic cleft of the communicating neurons.

Cocaine works by blocking the reuptake of the dopamine molecule through the transporter molecule that 'vacuums up' available dopamine from the synaptic cleft back into the pre-synaptic (transmitting) neuron (neuron upstream on the path of neurotransmission). The effect of 'vacuuming' the DA helps to end the chemical signal to the neuron next in line, and allows for a recovery of intact DA to make it available again for the transmission of another signal through its release in the synaptic cleft.

Normal Communication

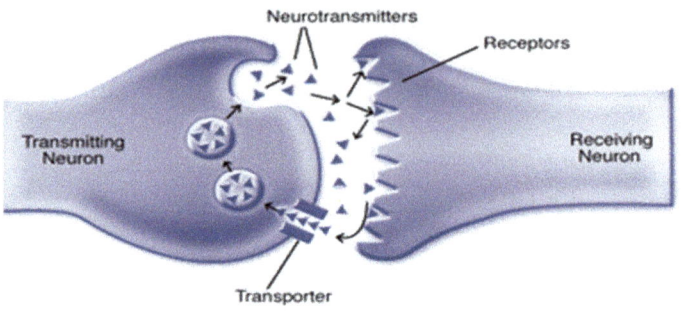

Communication When Cocaine Is Present

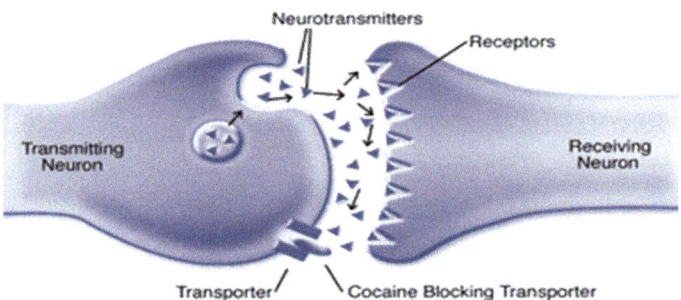

(Fig. 01 Adapted from NIDA Archive)
(https://archives.drugabuse.gov/news-events/nida-notes/1999/08/)
(cocaines-pleasurable-effects-may-involve-multiple-chemical-sites)

Amphetamines on the other hand, not only work like cocaine at blocking the reuptake of DA from the synaptic cleft, but they also cause dopamine (DA) stored in vesicles to be released into the synaptic cleft. This leads to a dramatic increase in the level of DA in the synaptic cleft as compared to the cocaine effect, while at the same time blocking the reuptake of dopamine back into the presynaptic (transmitting) neuron terminal. This leads to a substantially magnified and amplified effect of dopamine (DA) in the cleft compared with cocaine's effect and a much greater response in the postsynaptic (receiving) neuron under the effect of amphetamines and amphetamine salts such as Adderall®.

(**Fig. 02** Adapted from Presentation below)
(Action of cocaine is to block reuptake in DAT (dopamine transporter))
(Action of amphetamines is to block reuptake in DAT (dopamine transporter) and
Increase the release of dopamine from neuron terminal vesicles that store DA)
(From: Widely Prescribed Stimulants and the Risk of Psychosis in Young People with ADHD)

Methamphetamine provides an even stronger effect than amphetamine because methamphetamine is metabolized into amphetamine. As such, there is amphetamine-like activity from the methamphetamine followed by continued activity under the effect of the amphetamine that was a product of metabolism from the original ingested methamphetamine. Thus, methamphetamine has a substantially longer period of activity due to its presence, and then the continued presence of an active metabolite through the amphetamine, along the pathway of metabolism of the methamphetamine eventually into inert products.

Brain Regions Involved in ADHD:

The prefrontal cortex (PFC) region of the brain (the anterior most region of the brain above the eyebrows) has a heavy population of dopamine (DA) receptors as well as norepinephrine (NE) receptors. This region is important in attention regulation as well as working memory. The problem of dysfunction in the PFC region is thought to be linked to poor inhibition of behavior and plays a significant role in the problem of addiction. We have seen that a core definition of addiction is the objective evidence of dysfunctional behavior that continues despite the presence of adverse consequences. Therefore, poor functioning of the PFC region of the brain may well lead to repeated episodes of behavior out of control due to an underlying lack of emotional dampening allowing for the persistence of functioning through the meso-cortical limbic system.

There is research evidence, through structural imaging studies of patients with ADHD, to show that some common findings of smaller volumes in the dorsolateral PFC as well as in the region of the subcortical structures as well as the cerebellum **(13)(14)**. The dorsolateral PFC (dlPFC) is a region that is understood to be the so-called 'brakes' that allow for subcortical modulation of emotional states. In other words, a decrease in function of the dlPFC allows for a greater degree of emotional experience that may give rise to greater behavioral problems. The (L) dlPFC is the region typically treated with repetitive transcranial magnetic stimulation (rTMS), an outpatient office procedure that has been approved by the FDA for the treatment of clinically-resistant depressive symptoms. A decrease in functioning of the dlPFC is consistent with the heightened risk of addictive behavior. Furthermore, one group of researchers found that there was a fixed (i.e. stable, unchanging) overall brain volume decrease in ADHD patients from childhood through adolescence **(15)**. Another group of researchers also determined the reduction of inhibitory control in the dorsal anterior cingulate cortex (dACC), a region of the brain involved in the modulation of behavior **(16)**.

Brain imaging studies, such as functional magnetic resonance imaging (fMRI) and positron emission tomography (PET) scanning, in patients with ADHD support the hypothesis that there is a problem in the frontal-subcortical pathway feedback loop involved in motor control, behavioral inhibition and reward (dopamine) pathway modulation **(13)(17)(18)**. Such abnormalities can lead to an increased risk of aberrant behavior and the facilitated development of a substance use disorder.

Some environmental risks, such as maternal cigarette smoking (during pregnancy), low birth weight and prematurity, are associated with both ADHD and addiction (SUD).

The Impact of ADHD and SUD:

Studies have revealed that some 60% of patients with ADHD in childhood continue to have some functional symptoms into adulthood **(19)(20)(21)(22)**.

The combination of ADHD and substance use disorder (SUD) makes for more difficulty in treating either condition. The lack of treatment for one makes for a great deal of difficulty in the treatment of the other **(23)(24)(25)(26)(27)**. Both conditions require addressing a simultaneous treatment program.

Multiple studies have revealed an earlier onset of SUD in adolescents with a history of ADHD, particularly in those who exhibit hyperactive-impulsive tendencies **(28)(29)** as compared to those with inattentive ADHD symptoms **(30)**. A National comorbidity Survey Replication study revealed that patients with ADHD exhibited criteria for addiction in 15.2% as compared to a group of adolescents without ADHD symptomatology where the addiction rate was found to be 5.6% **(31)**. The presence of ADHD alone may lead to a 3-fold increase in the possibility of developing a SUD. Another study **(32)** also revealed that the onset of addiction was earlier for adolescents with ADHD, and even earlier for those who had an issue with conduct disorder. The cigarette smoking rate also seems to be increased in patients with ADHD **(33)(34)**. A large meta-analysis of 29 research studies evaluating the presence of ADHD in a population of adolescents and adults presenting with various SUDs revealed the presence of ADHD in almost a quarter (23%) of patients **(35)**.

ADHD alone has a substantial impact on general functioning. Children with ADHD who were followed into adulthood were found in one study to have completed less schooling, hold jobs that were less professional, suffer from poor self-esteem, exhibit social skill deficits and to be diagnosed with antisocial personality disorder (ASPD) **(36)**. Another study expanded on problems such as having been more likely to have a suspended driver's license, incurred more speeding fines, increased rate of job loss and multiple marriages **(37)**. ADHD placed these persons at greater risk not only for mood (depressive) and anxiety issues and ASPD but also for the development of SUD **(28)(36)(38)(39)(40)**. Women with ADHD are more susceptible to eating disorders **(41)**.

ADHD and SUD are individually coupled to higher rates of problematic behavior, emotional issues and poor self-esteem. The combination of ADHD and SUD likely make these problems more acute and the behavioral consequences even greater with a lower response to treatment **(24)(42)(43)**. Treatment should address both conditions concurrently.

Potential Link Between ADHD and SUD:

Because of the apparent clinically significant link between ADHD and the development of Sud, a number of studies have tried to determine the nature of the link between the two conditions.

One study addressing this interesting problem **(44)** suggested that the underlying seminal factor was the presence of a conduct disorder as part of the ADHD behavioral spectrum **(42)(45)(46)(47)**. Patients who revealed a conduct disorder were felt to have a higher risk of developing a SUD and at a younger age. Other studies have found that ADHD itself confers a higher risk for SUD independent of the conduct disorder component **(49)(50)**.

In either case, the presence of ADHD makes for a worse SUD condition with a worse prognosis **(42)(48)**. The factor of impulsivity, as an inability to control impulses, one that is commonly exhibited among ADHD patients, is a particular culprit in the acceleration of a SUD condition and a detriment to efforts at rehabilitation.

A significant concern regarding the link between ADHD and the higher risk of developing a SUD is whether exposure to stimulants, particularly in the developing brain of a child, could lead to an increased likelihood of developing a problem with drugs with a potent stimulatory effect. This heightened risk could occur through either a process of behavioral sensitization or the belief in a patient with ADHD that since they are prescribed pharmacologically potent stimulants for therapeutic purposes, they should not have a problem with recreational drugs such as cocaine, 'bath salts', 'ecstasy' or 'Molly'.

In a meta-analytic study, a study reviewing the results of a number of studies with a similar premise, the data did not reflect an increase in the risk of developing a SUD resulting from prescribed stimulants for ADHD. However, the risk was not reduced through treatment of ADHD with stimulants as had been proposed by a previous study **(51)**.

This meta-analytic study was followed by a longitudinal study, one that follows a group of patients over time, which found that there was an apparent protective effect from treatment of ADHD, particularly if treatment began at an early age **(52)**.

Recent studies report that earlier treatment and longer duration of treatment may be protective compared to no treatment **(53)(54)**. Further studies are required to provide for more secure conclusions.

Diagnosis of ADHD in the Addiction Population:

The recommendation for making the diagnosis of ADHD in a population of patients who already exhibit the symptom complex of SUD is to rely on a reliable screening instrument which would then necessarily be followed by a standardized diagnostic interview. We should not rely on screening instruments alone since the answers could be falsified when a person is motivated to acquire pharmacologic stimulants.

A greater level of difficulty is faced when trying to tease out an ADHD symptom complex from a patient with an active substance abuse condition. All decisions should be made with an open mind while entertaining the possibility that the underlying ADHD conditions exists while balancing any apparent motivation to qualify for prescription stimulants. Clinical assessment improves substantially if a patient could be abstinent for a minimum of 2-4 weeks. Of course, such conditions are not always easy to reach and the provider may be required to assess despite the ongoing use of substances of abuse.

(Adapted from Addiction Medicine 6th Ed)

References:

1. Faraone SV, et al. Molecular genetics of attention-deficit/hyperactivity disorder. Biol Psychiatry. 2005;57(11):1313-1323.

2. Sharp SI, McQuillin A, Gurling HM. Genetics of attention-deficit hyperactivity disorder (ADHD). Neuropharmacology. 2009;57(7-8):590-600.

3. Faraone SV, Biederman J. Neurobiology of attention-deficit hyperactivity disorder. Biol Psychiatry. 1998;44(10):951-958.

4. Thapar A, O'Donovan M, Owen MJ. The genetics of attention deficit hyperactivity disorder. Hum Mol Genet. 2005;14(Spec No. 2):R275-R282.

5. Dadds MR, et al. Epigenetic regulation of the DRD4 gene and dimensions of attention-deficit/hyperactivity disorder in children. Eur Child Adolesc Psychiatry. 2016;25(10):1081-1089.

6. Shook D, et al. Effect of dopamine transporter genotype on caudate volume in childhood ADHD and controls. Am J Med Genet B Neuropsychiatr Genet. 2011;156B(1):28-35.

7. Franklin TR, et al. Dopamine transporter genotype modulation of neural responses to smoking cues: confirmation in a new cohort. Addict Biol. 2011;16(2):308-322.

8. Grzywacz A, Samochowiec J. [Case–control, family based and screening for DNA sequence variation in the dopamine transporter gene polymorphism DAT 1 in alcohol dependence]. Psychiatr Pol. 2008;42(3):443-452.

9. National Institute on Alcohol Abuse and Alcoholism (NIAAA)

NIAAA - Drinking Levels Defined (Standards for Alcohol Consumption):

https://www.niaaa.nih.gov/alcohol-health/overview-alcohol-consumption/moderate-binge-drinking#:~:text=Heavy%20Alcohol%20Use%3A,than%207%20drinks%20per%20week

10. Christopher J. Morgan, Abdulla A.-B. Badawy, Alcohol-induced euphoria: exclusion of serotonin, Alcohol and Alcoholism, Volume 36, Issue 1, January 2001, Pages 22–25, https://doi.org/10.1093/alcalc/36.1.22

11. Lukas, S. E., Mendelson, J. H. and Benedikt, R. A. (1986) Instrumental analysis of ethanol-induced intoxication in human males. Psychopharmacology 89, 8-13.

12. Pettinati HM, O'Brien CP, Rabinowitz AR, Wortman SP, Oslin DW, Kampman KM, Dackis CA. The status of naltrexone in the treatment of alcohol dependence: specific effects on heavy drinking. J Clin Psychopharmacol. 2006 Dec;26(6):610-25.

    doi: 10.1097/01.jcp.0000245566.52401.20. PMID: 17110818.

13. Spencer TJ, Biederman J, Mick E. Attention-deficit/hyperactivity disorder: diagnosis, lifespan, comorbidities, and neurobiology. Ambul Pediatr. 2007;7(1 Suppl):73-81.

14. Seidman LJ, Valera EM, Makris N. Structural brain imaging of attention-deficit/hyperactivity disorder. Biol Psychiatry. 2005;57(11):1263-1272.

15. Castellanos FX, et al. Developmental trajectories of brain volume abnormalities in children and adolescents with

attention-deficit/hyperactivity disorder. JAMA. 2002;288(14):1740-1748.

16. Bush G, Valera EM, Seidman LJ. Functional neuroimaging of attention-deficit/hyperactivity disorder: a review and suggested future directions. Biol Psychiatry. 2005;57(11):1273-1284.

17. Alexander GE, DeLong MR, Strick PL. Parallel organization of functionally segregated circuits linking basal ganglia and cortex. Annu Rev Neurosci. 1986;9:357-381.

18. Volkow ND, et al. Dopamine in drug abuse and addiction: results of imaging studies and treatment implications. Arch Neurol. 2007;64(11):1575-1579.

19. Barkley R. *Attention-Deficit Hyperactivity Disorder*. 3rd ed. New York, NY: The Guilford Press, 2006:425-452.

20. Rasmussen P, Gillberg C. Natural outcome of ADHD with developmental coordination disorder at age 22 years: a controlled, longitudinal, community-based study. J Am Acad Child Adolesc Psychiatry. 2000;39(11):1424-1431.

21. Barkley RA, et al. The persistence of attention-deficit/hyperactivity disorder into young adulthood as a function of reporting source and definition of disorder. J Abnorm Psychol. 2002;111(2):279-289.

22. Biederman J, Mick E, Faraone SV. Age-dependent decline of symptoms of attention deficit hyperactivity disorder: impact of remission definition and symptom type. Am J

23. Mariani JJ, Levin FR. Treatment strategies for co-occurring ADHD and substance use disorders. Am J Addict. 2007;16(Suppl 1):45-54; quiz 55-56.

24. Carroll KM, Rounsaville BJ. History and significance of childhood attention deficit disorder in treatment-seeking cocaine abusers. Compr Psychiatry. 1993;34(2):75-82.

25. Levin FR, et al. Impact of attention-deficit hyperactivity disorder and other psychopathology on treatment retention among cocaine abusers in a therapeutic community. Addict Behav. 2004;29(9):1875-1882.

26. Stratton J, Gailfus D. A new approach to substance abuse treatment. Adolescents and adults with ADHD. J Subst Abuse Treat. 1998;15(2):89-94.

27. Sullivan M, Levin F. Attention deficit/hyperactivity disorder and substance abuse: diagnostic and therapeutic considerations. In: Adult Attention Deficit Disorder: Brain Mechanisms and Life Outcomes. New York, NY: New York Academy of Sciences, 2001.

28. Elkins IJ, McGue M, Iacono WG. Prospective effects of attention-deficit/hyperactivity disorder, conduct disorder, and sex on adolescent substance use and abuse. Arch Gen Psychiatry. 2007;64(10):1145-1152.

29. Chang Z, Lichtenstein P, Larsson H. The effects of childhood ADHD symptoms on early-onset substance use: a Swedish twin study. J Abnorm Child Psychol. 2012;40(3):425-435.

30. De Alwis D, et al. Attention-deficit/hyperactivity disorder subtypes and substance use and use disorders in NESARC. Addict Behav. 2014;39(8):1278-1285.

31. Kessler RC, et al. The prevalence and correlates of adult ADHD in the United States: results from the National Comorbidity Survey Replication. Am J Psychiatry. 2006;163(4):716-723.

32. Kessler RC, et al. Lifetime co-morbidity of DSM-IV disorders in the US National Comorbidity Survey Replication Adolescent Supplement (NCS-A). Psychol Med. 2012;42(9):1997-2010.

33. Pomerleau OF, et al. Cigarette smoking in adult patients diagnosed with attention deficit hyperactivity disorder. J Subst Abuse. 1995;7(3):373-378.

34. Tercyak KP, Lerman C, Audrain J. Association of attention-deficit/hyperactivity disorder symptoms with levels of cigarette smoking in a community sample of adolescents. J Am

35. van Emmerik-van Oortmerssen K, et al. Psychiatric comorbidity in treatment-seeking substance use disorder patients with and without attention deficit hyperactivity disorder: results of the IASP study. Addiction. 2014;109(2):262-272.

36. Mannuzza S, Klein RG. Long-term prognosis in attention-deficit/hyperactivity disorder. Child Adolesc Psychiatr Clin N Am. 2000;9(3):711-726.

37. Murphy KR, Barkley RA. Prevalence of DSM-IV symptoms of ADHD in adult licensed drivers: implications of clinical diagnosis. J Atten Disord. 1996;1:147-161.

38. Klein RG, et al. Clinical and functional outcome of childhood attention-deficit/hyperactivity disorder 33 years later. Arch Gen Psychiatry. 2012;69(12):1295-1303.

39. Greenfield B, Hechtman L, Weiss G. Two subgroups of hyperactives as adults: correlations of outcome. Can J Psychiatry. 1988;33(6):505-508.

40. Biederman J, et al. A randomized, placebo-controlled trial of OROS methylphenidate in adults with attention-

deficit/hyperactivity disorder. Biol Psychiatry. 2006;59(9):829-835.

41. Biederman J, et al. Adult psychiatric outcomes of girls with attention deficit hyperactivity disorder: 11-year follow-up in a longitudinal case-control study. Am J Psychiatry. 2010;167(4):409-417.

42. Wilens TE, Biederman J, Mick E. Does ADHD affect the course of substance abuse? Findings from a sample of adults with and without ADHD. Am J Addict. 1998;7(2):156-163.

43. Levin FR, et al. Bupropion treatment for cocaine abuse and adult attention-deficit/hyperactivity disorder. J Addict Dis. 2002;21(2):1-16.

44. Molina BS, Pelham WE Jr. Attention-deficit/hyperactivity disorder and risk of substance use disorder: developmental considerations, potential pathways, and opportunities for research. Annu Rev Clin Psychol. 2014; 10:607-639.

45. Gittelman R, et al. Hyperactive boys almost grown up. I. Psychiatric status. Arch Gen Psychiatry. 1985;42(10):937-947.

46. Thompson LL, et al. Contribution of ADHD symptoms to substance problems and delinquency in conduct-disordered adolescents. J Abnorm Child Psychol. 1996;24(3):325-347.

47. Milberger S, et al. Associations between ADHD and psychoactive substance use disorders. Findings from a longitudinal study of high-risk siblings of ADHD children. Am J Addict. 1997;6(4):318-329.

48. Biederman J, et al. Does attention-deficit hyperactivity disorder impact the developmental course of drug and alcohol abuse and dependence? Biol Psychiatry. 1998;44(4):269-273.

49. Mannuzza S, Klein RG, Addalli KA. Young adult mental status of hyperactive boys and their brothers: a prospective follow-up study. J Am Acad Child Adolesc Psychiatry. 1991;30(5):743-751.

50. Wilens TE, et al. Does ADHD predict substance-use disorders? A 10-year follow-up study of young adults with ADHD. J Am Acad Child Adolesc Psychiatry. 2011;50(6):543-553.

51. Faraone SV, Wilens T. Does stimulant treatment lead to substance use disorders? J Clin Psychiatry. 2003;64(Suppl 11):9-13.

52. Groenman AP, et al. Substance use disorders in adolescents with attention deficit hyperactivity disorder: a 4-year follow-up study. Addiction. 2013;108(8):1503-1511.

53. Chang Z, et al. Stimulant ADHD medication and risk for substance abuse. J Child Psychol Psychiatry. 2014;55(8):878-885.

54. McCabe SE, et al. Age of onset, duration, and type of medication therapy for attention-deficit/hyperactivity disorder and substance use during adolescence: a multi-Cohort National Study. J Am Acad Child Adolesc Psychiatry. 2016;55(6):479-486.

7

Universal Precautions in Prescribing Stimulants

(William Yvorchuk, MD CM)

A majority of patients appear to consume these controlled substance medications appropriately but there is a significant potential for misuse and abuse of these substances. We presently review a paradigm for "universal precautions" for stimulant medications with practical application in reducing the risks while promoting appropriate medication use.

Demographics:

ADHD is typically characterized by functional compromise due to high levels of inattention, overactivity, and impulsivity. ADHD appears to functionally affect some 5% of school-aged children and has been shown to also compromise some 4% of adults (**1,2,3**).

Universal Precautions Paradigm:

It is essentially impossible to predict with any degree of certainty who will become a problematic consumer of prescription-controlled substances or develop a substance use disorder *per se*. A paradigm was developed within the pain management community to avoid any prejudice in managing patients receiving long-term controlled substances under circumstances that may lead to misuse, high risk use, abuse or even substance dependence. Boundaries need to be established within the patient-physician relationship that can be applied objectively and without bias so as to provide the highest level of care for these patients within a relatively high-risk environment for controlled substance misuse.

As such, a parallel was drawn from past experience in identifying 'at risk' patients within the infectious disease model that is adapted to a biopsychosocial model that allows for an assessment of past or current aberrant behaviors, allowing for the application of reasonable and careful limits on the patient-physician relationship (**4**). The authors found it possible to triage chronic pain patients according to risk into several categories. Recommendations are then offered for further management and referral if necessary. This objective and respectful approach to assessment and management of the chronic pain patient can reduce stigma, improve patient care and mitigate risk (**4**).

Universal precautions in the infectious disease realm arose from a recognition that it was essentially impossible for the health care provider to reliably assess risk of infectivity during the initial assessment of a patient. After research into the prevalence and communicability of such chronic and contagious conditions such as Hepatitis B, C and HIV, the profession recognized that the safest, most objective and reasonable approach would be to apply an appropriate minimum level of precaution to all patients so as to reduce the risk of transmission to health care professionals caring for the patients. These 'universal precautions' are applied without prejudice to *all patients* and risk can later be stratified based on the patient's *functional* response to treatment, ongoing demeanor and behavior over time through the course of treatment.

The major concern to the healthcare professional when providing chronic care which includes the use of controlled substances that can be abused is the development of an addictive disorder. Addiction is essentially characterized as continued behavior despite the arising of problematic consequences to the patient and/or the patient's immediate family. There is no definitive test, cluster of signs or symptoms that predict who will do well on a therapeutic trial of opioids for chronic nonmalignant pain (CNMP) management. As such these authors first presented a minimum level of care applied to all patients presenting with CNMP.

The proposed recommendations follow below. They provide for improvement in the care of the patient, reduction of stigma as everyone is treated equally without bias and safety maximized as overall risk is mitigated. They are only meant to act as a starting point. A fluid ongoing evaluation through the course of the trial of treatment is imperative. It is particularly important to recognize the premise that use of controlled substances, opioids in the case of CNMP management, is to be considered an ongoing trial. The trial may end at any time if conditions arise whereby functional gain is no longer evident, medication misuse arises, or florid addiction develops. Patients with active addiction can still be treated but vigilance and monitoring are heightened for the *safety* of the patient. Careful reassessment is made on a visit-to-visit basis. On occasion, office visits may be required as often as weekly during a particularly acute phase.

Gourley's Proposed 10 Steps of Universal Precautions in Pain Medicine:

1. Make a diagnosis with appropriate differential diagnoses
2. Psychological assessment including risk of Addiction
3. Informed Consent including discussion of potential risks
4. Treatment Agreement - Expectations and Obligations of Patient and Provider
5. Pre- and Post- Intervention Assessment of Pain Level and *Function*
6. Appropriate Trial of Opioid Therapy and/or Adjunctive Medications
7. Reassessment of Pain Score and Level of Function
8. Continued reassessment of the Four 'A's: analgesia, activity, adverse effects, aberrant behavior
9. Periodically Review Pain Diagnosis and Comorbid Conditions, including SUDs
10. Careful and complete documentation

Universal Precautions to Reduce Stimulant Misuse in Treating Adult ADHD (5):

The inattention, impulsivity and hyperactivity associated with ADHD can functionally affect up to ~ 5% of school-aged children as well as ~ 4% of adults (**1,2,3**).

It is important to remember that we are discussing clinically relevant, functional deficiencies as a result of the symptom pathology of ADHD. We are not discussing improvements in well-being alone. Although prescription stimulants can improve virtually everyone in terms of increased endurance, focus, productivity and performance, the paradoxical response of a reduction of hyperactivity and impulsivity characterize the true ADHD patient. It is not unusual for such patients to report that they feel calmer and more at peace once having taken their prescription medication and relate the ability to go to sleep after a brief period of having taken the controlled stimulant medication. This is not true of the typical adult under the influence of stimulants. The use of stimulants can help such individuals stay up all night to study, work, drive and remain focused and productive.

Under the circumstances of substance abuse, many partyers inhale cocaine powder to help them stay awake and party well into the night and early morning hours. It is the person who has fallen asleep on the couch at the party after inhaling cocaine who is potentially the true ADHD patient.

Relevant Issues in Diagnosing ADHD:

According to the DSM-5 (**6**) diagnosis of ADHD requires the presence of symptoms prior to the age of 12 yr. (**7**). The age of onset criterion was based on data suggesting that nearly 90% of childhood ADHD symptoms began by the age of 12 yr. (**8**). As a result, the diagnosis of ADHD in adults was predicated on the report of some ADHD symptomatology present before age 12 and required accurate recall of symptoms by the adult patients in question. In order to improve for variance of recall in adult patients, the DSM-5 criteria (**6**) advise the treating physicians to validate only certain symptoms prior to the age of 12 rather than try to establish documentation of the full syndrome.

A difficulty in diagnosing ADHD in an adult who had not been diagnosed in childhood arises from the lack of reliable biomarkers or neuropsychological tests for diagnosis. Furthermore, most adult ADHD patients also present with at least one comorbidity (**6,9**). The focus of concern in adolescent and adult ADHD sufferers lies in the functional problems of inattention, difficulties with task completion, disorganization and issues with executive dysfunction (**5**). These skills play a vital role in performing at the level required to be a reliable and well-functioning adult in our society. Stimulants are *not* a suitable agent to help one 'get out of bed in the morning', 'have energy' to complete activities of daily living (ADLs), experience euphoria, 'stay up late' or 'have the energy' to 'get things done'.

Further complicating the issue of adult ADHD is the challenge on the neurodevelopmental concept of ADHD (**7**) presented by multiple studies that suggest that ADHD may develop *de novo* in adolescents (10) (11) and in adults (**12**) (**13**) (**14**). However, another study opposes this late-onset concept in associating these apparent late-onset symptoms co-occurring with other psychiatric disturbances (**15**). In other words, according to these authors (**15**), most of the symptoms of ADHD that purportedly initiated after 12 yr. could better be explained by *other* psychiatric disorders.

One of the comments in the paper by Modesto-Lowe (**5**), suggests that "available ADHD guidelines suggest that children and adults who respond to pharmacotherapy should continue it as long as it remains effective" (**10**). An issue of concern necessarily follows - what should we consider effectiveness of the medication. Is it of functional benefit, an emotional one or is it merely the desire to avoid the dysphoria of an acute or post-acute (prolonged) stimulant withdrawal state after years of prescription stimulant use and having developed physiologic dependence. Clearly, with the concerns for stimulant misuse and abuse, the correct practice of applied 'universal precautions' in the treatment of ADHD in adults demands a measurable *functionally*-based emphasis to justify the continued use of such controlled substances on a chronic basis. Mere emotional well-being is not a valid criterion for the continued use of a controlled substance with abuse potential.

Poor Recall by Adults of Childhood ADHD Symptoms:

A study conducted by a group (**16**) assessed the reliability of recall (retrospective report) of psychological and other symptoms compared to prospective measures in a population of 18yo patients who had been prospectively studied since birth. The findings revealed that recall of psychosocial variables "revealed the lowest level of agreement between prospective and retrospective measures" and that "reliance on retrospective reports about psychosocial variables should be approached with caution".

One study that had followed-up on patients after some 16 years, found that of all adults retrospectively given a diagnosis of childhood ADHD, only 27% actually had the disorder (in childhood) (**11**). The inference is that adult patients with purported ADHD and given the retrospective diagnosis of childhood ADHD based solely on *self-report* are *not* usually valid. This becomes concerning if providers are relying on self-report of childhood ADHD, at least in part, on making the diagnosis of adult ADHD.

An early prospective study (**12**) was conducted and followed 101 male adolescents (aged 16-23 yr.) who were diagnosed with ADHD in childhood (ages 6 to 12 yr.) compared with an equal number of normal controls (100 controls). Full ADHD syndrome only persisted in 31% of the patients.

A large study (**7**) of individuals followed from childhood to adulthood was designed to assess the reliability of recall of ADHD symptoms in a large cohort of adult patients. At age 22, some 3810 individuals were "assessed through structured interviews by trained psychologists regarding mental health outcomes, including ADHD diagnosis and ADHD symptoms in childhood". The retrospective recall was compared with available ADHD childhood symptoms at age 11. The result was that recall of childhood ADHD symptoms at the age of 22 compared to known information at the age of 11 had an accuracy of only 55.4%, with a sensitivity of 32.8% and a positive predictive value of 40.7%. In conclusion, these authors reported that the "recall of childhood ADHD symptoms seems an unreliable method to characterize the neurodevelopmental trajectory in adults with currently-impairing ADHD symptomatology". They specifically reported that "The performance of the self-report recalls to define the presence of several symptoms (of ADHD) before the age of twelve in an individual presenting a currently-impairing ADHD syndrome was extremely poor, demonstrating both low sensitivity and specificity due to high false positive and false negative rates. Also, there were no clinical characteristics strongly associated with false or true-recall of childhood symptoms that could help clinicians to raise red flags in order to judge the quality of the self-reported retrospective remembrance better".

A study was conducted in twin veterans (17) to examine whether the clinical course of ADHD was comparable to that observed in samples of children and adolescents. Furthermore, the study focused on the "utility of adult reports of lifetime ADHD symptoms by examining the heritability of retrospectively reported childhood symptoms". The results revealed that prevalence rates were consistent with those observed in other studies along with a "longitudinal decline in symptoms severity" with age. They also report that assessing ADHD in adults is less accurate than with children and adolescents. The authors also report that "Some researchers argue that retrospective diagnoses of childhood ADHD made on the basis of self-reports, particularly for an older adult, would, in most cases, be difficult to establish (18)(19). They argue that inaccuracies and difficulties in remembering early childhood signs and symptoms are probable. We do not dispute the plausibility of this position."

The results of a recent longitudinal study were presented in late 2020 (**20**) on an evaluation of retrospective reports by adults with purported ADHD based on their recall (self-ratings) as compared for accuracy to parents or significant others (proxy ratings) along with the influence of current ADHD symptom severity and ADHD-associated impairments on retrospective symptom ratings. Participants were members of a study who had been diagnosed and treated for ADHD during childhood and then again reassessed in adulthood when 22 to 32 years of age (18-year F/U). "Both self- and proxy ratings of *adult* ADHD were substantially and significantly lower than parent ratings of ADHD collected in childhood suggesting that ADHD symptoms *lessened* from childhood to adulthood. Also consistent with previous evidence (**21**), proxy ratings of hyperactivity-impulsivity showed a substantially greater decline over time compared to ratings of inattention." Furthermore, the authors relate that "We therefore conclude that our data confirm previous findings of a *developmental reduction in ADHD symptomatology* (**22**)".

Multiple studies have found that adult patients report more ADHD symptoms than do parents or other informants (**23,24**). The aforementioned authors (**20**) report the demonstration "that participants' retrospective symptom recall was associated with the severity of current ADHD symptoms. This finding fits well with the concept of a *state-dependent recall*, which postulates that recall of past symptoms and episodes is affected by a patient's emotional and physical state at the time of recall (**25**). The relationship between current distress and recall of past emotions or symptoms has previously been supported by evidence of a *negative recall bias* in patients with depression (**26**), panic disorders (**27**), borderline personality disorder (**28**), or acute pain (**29**)." They also report that "the present findings demonstrate that cross-informant agreement for retrospective ratings of childhood ADHD is *at most* moderate, and therefore support the recommendation of the European Network Adult ADHD (ENAA) that information from different sources should be used when diagnosing ADHD in adults (**30**).

Age-Dependent Decline of Symptoms of ADHD:

There has been a general impression that the symptoms of childhood ADHD tend to decline over time.

The early ADHD-like findings of inattention, hyperactivity, lack of emotional modulation, compulsivity is ubiquitous among preschoolers and grade school children. The fine line of demarcation between that of a pathologic condition and those of active childhood are primarily based on functional impairment. This demarcation can become ambiguous at times. Whether the functional issues arise from an innate pathology within the child or from life circumstances in the environment can be difficult to discern.

One facet of the course of this disease over an early lifetime with which there is general agreement is the fact that functionally compromising symptoms appear to abate over time and remain limited once adulthood is reached.

A major reason for this apparent decline of functionally compromising symptoms is the natural development and maturation of the human brain over the first few decades of life.

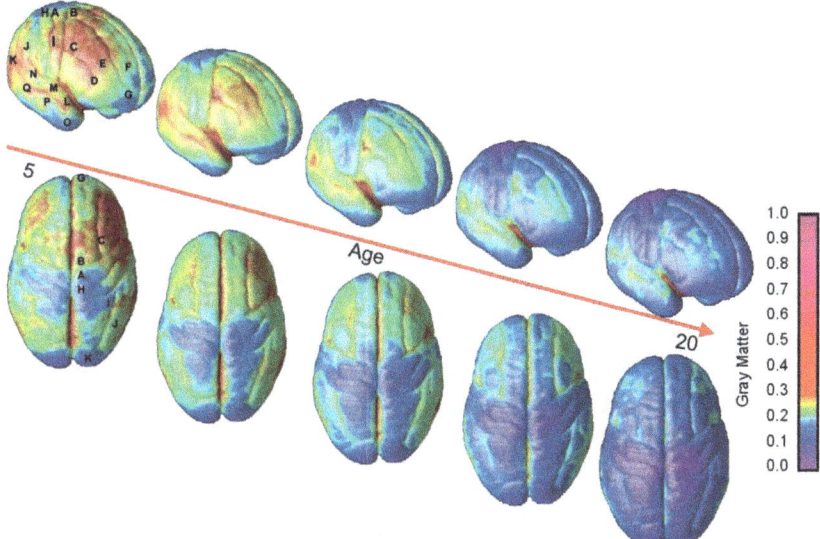

Fig 1. Right lateral and top views of the dynamic sequence of gray matter maturation over the cortical surface. The side bar shows a color representation in units of Gray Matter volume. Adapted from (**31**) **Gogtay et al (2004)**.

Gray matter of the human brain matures over the first 3 decades of life. The occipital lobe, the structure that houses our visual center matures first by around the age of 5. This is one of the reasons for which we are so dominated by our visual sense. Most humans discern information in their environment through the visual sense. We tend to be dominated by visual input. Of the information we discern and input from our environment, some 90% is taken in through the visual sense. Visual perception is one of the major reasons we perceive ourselves to be separate and individuated human beings thus developing a sense of self, a 'me'. We tend to begin to discern ourselves in the mirror around 20 months of age (mirror self-recognition (MSR) test). Our early development of self-identification with a sense of 'self', a stream of consciousness in the mind coupled with an experience of time is first established around the age of 8. The adolescent brain continues to mature but the limbic system matures before the frontal cortex region. As such, adolescents are far more emotional as compared to a mature adult in their mid-20's when the prefrontal cortex matures thus providing for the experience of a mature sense of 'self' in the world as well as maturation of the dorsolateral prefrontal cortex region where our functional emotional braking system lies.

Decline in number of neurons after birth- as though the immature, new brain collapses into the functional egoic 'me-nome'.

The left dorsolateral prefrontal cortex (dlPFC) is the region where repetitive Transcranial Magnetic Stimulation (rTMS) (**32**)(**33**) can be applied to substantially improve depression resistant to other means including antidepressant medications, and psychological interventions, coping techniques and skills.

The emotional component of our internal experience is dampened with increasing activity in the region of the dlPFC influencing the subcortical structures, including the region of the VTA which is an initiating site in the midbrain on the activity of the dopaminergic reward pathways. rTMS acts by stimulating activity (neuronal firing) in the dlPFC which then sends glutaminergic signals through the midbrain and other subcortical structures as a dampening effect, a negative feedback modulation system. The greater the activity in the dlPFC, then the greater the dampening effect on the emotional subcortical pathways, therefore reducing the experience of depression as well as anxiety. Depression functionally arises as an ongoing, pervasive and preconscious sense of victimization from previous life experience to the present. Whereas anxiety arises as a projection of victimization from the past into the future.

In the majority of cases, addiction is driven by anxiety, a projected victimization into the future which is yet to happen and can be more easily modulated. Anxiety essentially arises as a fabrication, an expected experience of victimization at some time in the future. Because future experience has yet to occur, anxiety is malleable and more amenable to influence through psychogenically active (addictive) substances.

Depression arises from past experience of victimization that remains less amenable to emotional shifts through chemical use. Depression may also be coupled with a greater sense of despair which may therefore lead to suicidal ideation.

In states of profound emotional turbulence, depression is coupled more with suicidality whereas anxiety is coupled more to addiction and excessive (at risk) substance use.

. . . .

The arising of a mature dlPFC with emotional dampening may help explain the reduction in functional problems and the lessening of overt, classic ADHD symptomatology. The mature brain reveals greater emotional modulation and is less driven to functional compromise from underlying emotional fluctuations.

This condition of greater emotional modulation may help to explain much of the reduction in functional compromise with ADHD in adults. Multiple studies have reported on the decline of ADHD symptoms as patients move into adulthood (xxx).

. . . .

A longitudinal study (**34**) was developed to investigate the adult sequelae of the childhood ADHD disorder. The follow-up intervals ranged from 13 to 19 years.

The authors found that childhood ADHD tends to predict specific adult psychiatric disorders, namely antisocial and drug abuse disorders. In the *adolescent* outcome of this particular cohort, they found that these disturbances were dependent on the *continuation* of ADHD symptoms. In contrast, in *adulthood*, antisocial and drug disorders appeared, in part, *independent* of sustained ADHD.

This study was reviewed some 5 years later (**35**). The authors found the presence of significantly higher prevalence of antisocial personality disorder (12% versus 3%) and nonalcohol substance abuse (12% versus 4%) in the probands (clinically followed individuals), whereas mood disorders (4% versus 4%) and anxiety disorders (2% versus 7%) were not significantly different. At *adult follow-up*,

ADHD was *rare*, occurring in only 4% of the probands. They reported that children with ADHD are at significantly higher risk for a specific negative course marked by antisocial and substance-related disorders.

Another study followed ADHD children to determine their long-term clinical prognosis (**36**). The authors attempted to trace the developmental course of ADHD from childhood to adulthood. They found that many of the patients had quite a "bumpy road They found that, in "early and middle adolescence, relative deficits are seen in academic and social functioning". The classic ADHD symptoms remained a problem in some 2/3 to ¾ of the affected children, whereas antisocial behaviors, in some cases amounting to Conduct Disorder, were common. Many of the difficulties persisted into the late adolescence where "Deficits continue to be observed in academic and social domains (lower grades, more courses failed, worse performance on standardized tests, fewer friends, and rated less adequate in psychosocial adjustment). Some 2/5 continued to experience ADHD symptoms to a clinically significant degree. ¼ to 1/3 revealed diagnosed antisocial disorder, and 2/3 of these were arrested. Drug abuse was observed in a significant minority.

Once in the mid-20s, dysfunctions remained apparent in these same areas. However, some were able to achieve higher degrees of education and a full 2/3 of the children showed "no evidence of any mental disorder in adulthood". They concluded that "although ADHD children, as a group, fare poorly compared with their non-ADHD counterparts, the childhood syndrome does not preclude attaining high educational and vocational goals, and *most children no longer exhibit clinically significant* emotional or behavioral problems once they reach their mid-twenties."

In a meta-analysis of ADHD follow-up studies to examine the persistence of ADHD into adulthood (**37**), a group concluded that "estimates of persistence of ADHD rely heavily on how one defines persistence. Yet, regardless of definition, (the) analyses show that evidence for ADHD lessens with age."

Another meta-analysis reviewing the same problem of retention (or lack thereof) of ADHD symptoms from childhood into adulthood (**38**) re-examined patients from 4 to 16 years after their diagnosis "to determine the level of retained ADHD". One result was that "The data followed an *exponential decline* over time to a *high degree of accuracy*". The conclusion drawn was that "The rate of ADHD in a given age group appears to decline by 50% approximately every 5 years. If a prevalence of ADHD in childhood of 4% is assumed and the exponential decline extrapolated, the estimated rate of adult ADHD ranges from about 0.8% at age 20 to 0.05% at age 40". This is a marked decline of ADHD symptomatology over time.

A group well acquainted with the study of ADHD patients looked at the age-dependent decline in ADHD symptoms from childhood to adulthood with a focus on the clinical nature of the remission process (**39**). Symptom decline in ADHD was examined with *different* definitions of remission. Some 128 boys were assessed 5 times over 4 years. They looked at the prevalence of symptoms at a measure of that which was less than full syndrome; less than subthreshold diagnosis; and full recovery remission. The prevalence of each was estimated as a function of age. A primary result was the finding that age alone "was significantly associated with decline in total ADHD symptoms and symptoms of hyperactivity, impulsivity, and inattention. Symptoms of *inattention* remitted for fewer subjects than did symptoms of hyperactivity or impulsivity". "The proportion of subjects experiencing remission varied considerably with the definition used". Therefore, the results may indicate "that differences in reported remission rates reflect the definition used rather than the disorder's course." The results also provide for the premise and clinical observation that hyperactivity and impulsivity symptoms tend to decline at a higher rate than inattention symptoms.

In yet another 10-year prospective study by the same group (**40**) and looking at the lifetime prevalence of overall psychopathology in a sample of youth with and without ADHD, they found that "lifetime prevalence for all categories of psychopathology was significantly greater in ADHD young adults". ADHD youth were found to be "at high risk for a wide range of adverse psychiatric outcomes including markedly elevated rates of antisocial, addictive, mood and anxiety disorders".

The plethora and variety of psychopathology in ADHD subjects are compounded and worsened with the use of controlled stimulant substances in adolescence and adulthood.

ADHD and SUDs:

It is relatively well understood and accepted that ADHD leads to significant functional compromise as well as psychopathologic circumstances that lead to a higher rate of addiction and substance abuse (high risk use) in adolescents and young adults.

The development of a SUD on the background of ADHD complicates both the assessment (diagnosis and assessment of the degree of functional impairment) and treatment of each disorder. These commonly comorbid conditions compromise the patient at a profound level and significantly reduce the rates of remission for each condition. In particular, addiction is more profound with higher relapse rates and greater resistance to change along with difficulty in following instructions as well as participating in the various functions of recovery from addiction such as group participation, psychological techniques of relapse prevention, application of coping skills, avoidance of lapse or relapse from substance use, compromised ability to process emotional stressors along with limited capacity to endure emotional discomfort, participate in formal recovery practice and maintain composure under duress.

An early study by a group well-versed in ADHD pathology (**41**)(**42**) evaluated the association between ADHD and psychoactive substance addiction in adults with ADHD. Some 120 adults with established childhood onset of ADHD were compared with some 268 non-ADHD symptomatic adults.

The results revealed evidence for a higher lifetime risk of SUD in ADHD adults (52%) compared with non-ADHD adults (27%). Interestingly, the two groups did not differ in the rate of alcohol use disorders. However, the ADHD adults had significantly higher rates of drug and drug + alcohol use disorders than the control subjects. The authors also report that "ADHD significantly increased the risk for substance use disorders *independently* of a psychiatric comorbidity". Furthermore, as seen in other studies, the "presence of Antisocial disorders significantly increased the risk for substance use disorders independently of ADHD status."

In summary, psychiatric comorbidity increased the risk for psychoactive substance use disorders in adults with ADHD. However, it was also found that "by itself ADHD was a significant risk factor for substance use disorders".

A study (43) was conducted on subjects with ADHD focusing on the age of onset of psychoactive substance addiction in adults with ADHD. Group comparisons were made between the age of onset and the Cox Proportional Hazard model to examine the development of SUD over time. A major finding was that of "ADHD associated with earlier onset of PSUD independently of psychiatric comorbidity." Furthermore, "conduct disorder and juvenile bipolar disorder conferred a significantly increased risk for early onset PSUD independently of ADHD." Another observation was the finding of "psychiatric disorders commonly emerged before the onset of PSUD in both groups."

Persistent ADHD with and without psychiatric comorbidity was associated with adolescent onset substance addiction. Not surprisingly, "comorbidity with conduct and juvenile bipolar disorders predicted very early onset addiction."

A longitudinal study focusing on the comorbidity of ADHD and SUD of high-risk siblings of ADHD children (44) found that 4-year follow-up, ADHD and male gender predicted higher rates and an earlier onset of psychoactive substance addiction. The results further defined that the risk was particularly high if the siblings had ADHD plus conduct disorder.

It appears that a greater rate and degree of pathology of substance addiction in patients with ADHD is significantly worsened with the comorbidity of conduct disorder.

In a study (45) performed with a focus on ADHD influencing the course of the recovery of addiction in an individual with comorbid conditions, the authors examined the effects of ADHD and psychiatric comorbidity on the recovery from psychoactive substance addiction (PSUD).

The authors reported that "Although PSUD remitted in 80% of both groups, the rate of remission and duration of PSUD was quite different in the ADHD vs. non-ADHD subjects. The duration of PSUD was 37.2 months longer in the ADHD than in non-ADHD subjects. The median time to PSUD remission was more than twice as long in ADHD than in control subjects (144 vs. 60 months, respectively). ADHD is associated with a longer duration of PSUD and a significantly slower remission rate."

It not only appears that ADHD has a serious influence on the development of a substance use disorder, but as suspected will significantly compromise the patient's ability to secure recovery.

In another article focused on ADHD and substance abuse (46), patterns of association of the comorbid conditions are considered. With the perspective that some 50% of patients with persistent ADHD develop addiction, and that ADHD appears to present an independent risk factor for the development of a SUD, they reviewed the clinical challenges posed by the diagnosis of ADHD in substance-abusing populations.

Results included the finding that nicotine dependence was substantially more common among adults with ADHD (40%) than in the general population (26%).

According to the authors "The presence of ADHD may also affect the course of adolescent substance abuse in several ways: predicting earlier age of onset, longer duration of substance-use disorder, and progression of alcohol abuse to another drug-use disorder. Individuals with ADHD have been noted to have a shorter interval between the onsets of drug abuse and drug dependence. Such individuals are also at greater risk for treatment failure, as their disruptive behaviors interfere with treatment access and response."

(If not already discussed - consider some studies on Rx of ADHD to also improve recovery)

. . . .

The application of universal precautions helps both the physician and the patient directly. The physician can feel more comfortable in prescribing controlled substances over time and the patient has the benefit of a structured framework to assist with appropriate medication use and a clear paradigm of expectations in routine monitoring.

A proposal for Universal Precautions in the application for stimulants prescribed for adult ADHD (**47**) are reminiscent of the principles applied to the prescribing of opioids for CNMP and include:

1. Careful diagnosis

   j. high scores on routine screening tools must be interpreted in the clinical context of the patient's overall presentation
   k. ADHD symptoms should be exhaustively explored and should establish a basis of functional compromise for the patient. The functional improvement after having begun the medication regimen should be discussed and documented at each visit
   l. The diagnosis of adult ADHD requires evidence for symptoms in childhood. We have already seen that hindsight self-report cannot be trusted. The collection of valid collateral material can be time-consuming and burdensome
   m. Neuropsychological testing may be helpful in defining impairment(s)
   n. Level of function and impairment in several domains should be elucidated and documented thoroughly allowing for comparison of valid functional improvement over the course of the individualized medication trial
   o. The ongoing use of stimulants should be considered an ongoing trial of treatment that is reviewed at each visit and the functional aspects documented. Once there is either a loss of functional improvement or evidence of a deterioration in function ensues, the trial should be immediately reevaluated, and the controlled substance possibly tapered or terminated

2. Assessment of comorbid states

    a. Comorbid conditions are the rule and the norm in adults with ADHD

    b. Comorbid conditions range from anxiety, depression and SUD to social phobia, PTSD and Antisocial Personality Disorder (9)(48)

    c. They need to be teased out thoroughly because these pathologies often influence compliance to a treatment program to a substantial degree

3. Baseline risk stratification for stimulant misuse (49) (?50)(51?)

    a. Short-acting stimulants have a higher risk for misuse

    b. Sudden dopamine surges (phasic dopamine increase) is substantially more reinforcing than therapeutic dopamine release (52)

    c. Extended-release formulations provide for a steadier and sustained level of symptom relief through protracted levels of therapeutic dopamine release (53)

4. Informed consent processes

    a. Through proper disclosure patients may have a better appreciation for risk v benefit concerns as well as an improvement in expectations, thus helping to mitigate unreasonable expectations with respect to the likelihood of receiving a prescription for a stimulant against functional improvement and proper medication use (54)

    b. The abuse potential and addictive nature of the medications are addressed

c. The premise of considering the treatment program as an ongoing trial rather than an indefinite expectation of the 'reward' of a controlled substance prescription

d. The parameters for cessation of a particular medication treatment and alternatives are also addressed

5. Treatment agreement

   a. These are needed prior to initiating treatment with controlled substances (55)(56)

   b. These assist in the disclosure of parameters and boundaries to the ongoing use of controlled (Schedule II) substances for treatment

   c. Issues of diversion and abuse liability as well as alternative treatments and nontreatment are discussed

   d. Proper and safe storage of the medication is discussed

   e. Required periodic in person follow-up, urine drug testing (UDT), pharmacy protocol, management of stolen or 'lost' medication, and avoidance of doctor shopping are addressed (56)

   f. Patient commitment and compliance in a diligent and rigorously monitored treatment plan are reinforced as a pre-requisite for continued prescribing of controlled substance stimulants

   g. The protocol reinforces a perspective of safety for the patient and others

6. Periodic reassessments of treatment response

   a. Both symptom control and functional improvement are highlighted

b. Functional goals need to be set and met to continue with the medication trial (57)
c. Lack of improvement, or the lack of maintenance of functional improvement, requires reassessment of the therapeutic trial

7. Meticulous documentation and monitoring

a. Different levels of vigilance will be required for different patients depending on their level of function, adherence to the program, medication habits, and the like
b. Documentation should be as complete as possible under the circumstances of practice
c. Review of state prescription drug monitoring program (PDMP); Patterns of drug use or misuse will become evident over time
d. Functional goals agreed upon by provider and patient at time of initiation of trial require ongoing evaluation, monitoring and documentation (57)

8. The four 'A's in ADHD patient monitoring (47):

a. ADHD symptom tracking; self-report scales can be very misleading
b. ADLs - activities of daily living; collateral information from family members, peers, workplace can be marked importance
c. Adverse events - Vital signs, GI issues, headache, aggression, anxiety, depression, sleeping habits, delusions, psychosis
d. Aberrant behavior - medication misuse, abuse, diversion; pill counts, UDTs, PDMP results

Treatment agreements are particularly useful if behavioral aberrancies arise and the medication trial requires an amendment or termination.

Cultural Issues:

As a culture, we need to avoid reinforcing the premise of 'a pill for every ill' along with the expectation that we need to modulate our emotional state with controlled substance medications.

Controlled substances are fraught with potentially devastating side effects, some of which lead directly to our prompt demise.

The use of controlled substances should be reserved for use over brief periods, under close supervision and avoidance of the expectation that their use will be a lifelong commitment.

It has become apparent that the US, making up ~ 4.4-4.6% of the world's population, consumes over 80% of the world's opioids (**58**) including 99% of the world's supply of hydrocodone as well as 2/3 of the world's supply of illicit substances (**59**).

We have reached the crisis point. Our cultural decline under these circumstances is inevitable. The questions remain, how quickly will we succumb, and can we possibly begin a recovery from our dependence on controlled substances for emotional modulation.

References:

1. Polanczyk G, de Lima MS, Horta BL, Biederman J, Rohde LA. The worldwide prevalence of ADHD: a systematic review and metaregression analysis. Am J Psychiatry 2007; 164:942-948.

2. Polanczyk GV, Wilcutt EG, Salum GA, Kieling C, Rohde LA. ADHD prevalence estimates across three decades: an updated system- atic review and meta-regression analysis. Int J Epidemiol 2014; 43:434-442.

3. Wilens TE. ADHD: Prevalence, diagnosis, and issues of comorbidity. CNS Spectr 2007; 12(suppl 6):1-5.

4. Gourlay DL, Heit HA, Almahrezi A. Universal precautions in pain medicine. Pain Med 2005;6:107-12.9

5. Modesto-Lowe V, Meyer A, Soovajian V. A clinician's guide to adult attention-deficit hyperactivity disorder. Conn Med 2012; 76:517-523.

6. American Psychiatric Association (2013) *Diagnostic and Statistical Manual of Mental Disorders: DSM-5*, 5th edn. Washington, DC: American Psychiatric Association, American Psychiatric Publishing

7. Breda V, Rohde LA, Menezes AMB, Anselmi L, Caye A, Rovaris DL, Vitola ES, Bau CHD, Grevet EH (2020). Revisiting ADHD age-of-onset in adults: to what extent should we rely on the recall of childhood symptoms? *Psychological Medicine* 50, 857-866.

   https:// doi.org/10.1017/S003329171900076X

8. Kieling C, Kieling RR, Rohde LA, Frick PJ, Moffitt T, Nigg JT, Tannock R and Castellanos FX (2010) The age at onset

of attention deficit hyperactiv- ity disorder. *The American Journal of Psychiatry* 167, 14-16.

9. Kessler RC, Adler L, Barkley R, et al. The prevalence and correlates of adult ADHD in the United States: results from the National Co- morbidity Survey Replication. Am J Psychiatry 2006; 163:716-723.

10. Todd RD, Huang H and Henderson CA (2008) Poor utility of the age of onset criterion for DSM-IV attention deficit/hyperactivity disorder: recom- mendations for DSM-V and ICD-11. *Journal of Child Psychology and Psychiatry and Allied Disciplines* 49, 942-949.

11. Lecendreux M, Konofal E, Cortese S and Faraone SV (2015) A 4-year follow-up of attention-deficit/hyperactivity disorder in a population sample. *Journal of Clinical Psychiatry* 76, 712-719.

12. Lecendreux M, Konofal E, Cortese S and Faraone SV (2015) A 4-year follow-up of attention-deficit/hyperactivity disorder in a population sample. *Journal of Clinical Psychiatry* 76, 712-719.

13. Agnew-Blais JC, Polanczyk GV, Danese A, Wertz J, Moffitt TE and Arseneault L (2016) Evaluation of the persistence, remission, and emergence of attention-deficit/hyperactivity disorder in young adulthood. *JAMA Psychiatry* 73, 713-720.

14. Caye A, Rocha TBM, Anselmi L, Murray J, Menezes AMB, Barros FC, Gonçalves H, Wehrmeister F, Jensen CM, Steinhausen HC, Swanson JM, Kieling C and Rohde LA (2016) Attention-deficit/hyperactivity disorder tra- jectories from childhood to young adulthood evidence from a birth cohort supporting a late-onset syndrome. *JAMA Psychiatry* 73, 705-712.

15. Sibley MH, Rohde LA, Swanson JM, Hechtman LT, Molina BSG, Mitchell JT, Arnold LE, Caye A, Kennedy TM, Roy A, Stehli A, Vitiello B, Severe JB, Jensen PS, Hoagwood K, Richters J, Vereen D, Hinshaw SP, Elliott GR, Wells KC, Epstein JN, Murray DW, Conners CK, March J, Wigal T, Cantwell DP, Abikoff HB, Greenhill LL, Newcorn JH, Hoza B, Pelham WE, Gibbons RD, Marcus S, Hur K, Kraemer HC, Hanley T and Stern K (2018) Late-onset ADHD reconsidered with comprehensive repeated assessments between ages 10 and 25. *American Journal of Psychiatry* 175, 140-149

16. Henry B, Moffitt TE, Caspi A, Langley J and Silva PA (1994) On the 'remembrance of things past': a longitudinal evaluation of the Retrospective method. *Psychological Assessment* 6, 92-101.

17. Schultz MR, Rabi K, Faraone SV, Kremen W, Lyons MJ. Efficacy of retrospective recall of attention-deficit hyperactivity disorder symptoms: A twin study. Twin Res Hum Genet. 2006 Apr;9(2):220-32. doi: 10.1375/183242706776382374. PMID: 16611492.

18. Jackson, B., & Farrugia, D. (1997). Diagnosis and treatment of adults with attention deficit hyperactivity disorder. *Journal of Counseling and Development*, *75,* 55-62.

19. Shaffer, D. (1994). Attention deficit hyperactivity disorder in adults. *The American Journal of Psychiatry, 151*, 633-638.

20. von Wirth, E., Mandler, J., Breuer, D. *et al.* The Accuracy of Retrospective Recall of Childhood ADHD: Results from a Longitudinal Study. *J Psychopathol Behav Assess* **43,** 413-426 (2021). https://doi.org/10.1007/s10862-020-09852-1

21. Döpfner, M., Hautmann, C., Görtz-Dorten, A., Klasen, F., Ravens- Sieberer, U., & The BELLA study group. (2015).

Long-term course of ADHD symptoms from childhood to early adulthood in a community sample. *European Child & Adolescent Psychiatry, 24*, 665- 673.

22. Langberg, J. M., Epstein, J. N., Altaye, M., Molina, B. S. G., Arnold, L. E., & Vitiello, B. (2008). The transition to middle school is associated with changes in the developmental trajectory of ADHD symptomatology in young adolescents with ADHD. *Journal of Clinical Child & Adolescent Psychology, 37*, 651-663.

23. Magnússon, P., Smári, J., Baldursson, D. S., Kristjánsson, J. S., Sigurbjornsdóttir, S. H., & Guomundsson, O. O. (2006). Validity of self-report and informant rating scales of adult ADHD symptoms in comparison with a semistructured diagnostic interview. *Journal of Attention Disorders, 9*(3), 494-503.

24. Murphy, P., & Scharchar, R. (2000). Use of self-ratings in the assessment of symptoms of attention hyperactivity disorder in adults. *American Journal of Psychiatry, 157*, 1156-1159.

25. Barsky, A. J. (2002). Forgetting, fabricating and telescoping: The insta- bility of the medical history. *Archives of Internal Medicine, 162*(9), 981-984.

26. Ben-Zeev, D., & Young, M. A. (2010). Accuracy of hospitalized de- pressed patients' and healthy controls' retrospective symptom re- ports. *Journal of Nervous and Mental Disease, 198*, 280-285.

27. Margraf, J., Taylor, C. B., Ehlers, A., Roth, W. T., & Agras, W. S. (1987). Panic attacks in the natural environment. *Journal of Nervous and Mental Diseases, 175*, 558-565.

28. Ebner-Priemer, U. W., Kuo, J., Welch, S. S., Thielgen, T., Witte, S., Bohus, M., & Linehan, M. M. (2006). A valence-

dependent group-specific recall bias of retrospective self-reports. *Journal of Nervous and Mental Disease, 194*, 775-779.

29. Eich, E., Reeves, J. L., Jaeger, B., & Graff-Radford, S. B. (1985). Memory for pain: Relation between past and present pain intensity. *Pain, 23*(4), 375-380.

30. Kooij, J. J. S., Bijlenga, D., Salerno, L., et al. (2019). Updated European consensus statement on diagnosis and treatment of adult ADHD. *European Psychiatry, 56*, 14-34.

31. Gogtay, N., Giedd, J. N., Lusk, L., Hayashi, K. M., Greenstein, D., Vaituzis, A. C., ... Thompson, P. M. (2004). Dynamic mapping of human cortical development during childhood through early adulthood. *Proceedings of the National Academy of Sciences of the United States of America, 101*(21), 8174-8179.

https://doi.org/10.1073/pnas.0402680101

32. Padberg F, Zwanzger P, Keck ME, Kathmann N, Mikhaiel P, Ella R, Rupprecht P, Thoma H, Hampel H, Toschi N, Möller HJ. Repetitive transcranial magnetic stimulation (rTMS) in major depression: relation between efficacy and stimulation intensity. Neuropsychopharmacology. 2002 Oct;27(4):638-45. doi: 10.1016/S0893-133X(02)00338-X. PMID: 12377400.

33. Rizvi S, Khan AM. Use of Transcranial Magnetic Stimulation for Depression. *Cureus*. 2019;11(5):e4736. Published 2019 May 23. doi:10.7759/cureus.4736

34. Mannuzza, S., Klein, R. G., Bessler, A., Malloy, P., & LaPadula, M. (1993). Adult outcome of hyperactive boys: Educational achievement, occupational rank, and psychiatric status. *Archives of General Psychiatry,*

35. Mannuzza S, Klein RG, Bessler A, Malloy P, LaPadula M. Adult psychiatric status of hyperactive boys grown up. *Am J Psychiatry*. 1998 Apr;155(4):493-8. doi: 10.1176/ajp.155.4.493. PMID: 9545994.

36. Mannuzza S, Klein RG. Long-term prognosis in attention-deficit/hyperactivity disorder. *Child Adolesc Psychiatr Clin N Am*. 2000 Jul;9(3):711-26. PMID: 10944664.

37. Faraone, S., Biederman, J., & Mick, E. (2006). The age dependent decline of attention-deficit/hyperactivity disorder: A meta-analysis of follow-up studies. *Psychological Medicine*.

38. Hill JC, Schoener EP. Age-dependent decline of attention deficit hyperactivity disorder. Am J Psychiatry. 1996 Sep;153(9):1143-6. doi: 10.1176/ajp.153.9.1143. PMID: 8780416.

39. Biederman, J., Mick, E., & Faraone, S. V. (2000). Age-dependent decline of symptoms of ADHD: Impact of remission definition and symptom type. *American Journal of Psychiatry, 157*, 816-818.

40. Biederman, J., Monuteaux, M., Mick,E., Spencer, T., wilens, t., Silva, J., . . . Faraone, S. (2006). Young adult outcome of attention deficit hyperactivity disorder: A controlled 10-year follow-up study. Psychological Medicine, 36(2), 167-179. doi:10.1017/S0033291705006410

41. Biederman J, Wilens T, Mick E, Milberger S, Spencer TJ, Faraone SV. Psychoactive substance use disorders in adults with attention deficit hyperactivity disorder (ADHD): effects of ADHD and psychiatric comorbidity. Am J Psychiatry. 1995 Nov;152(11):1652-8. doi: 10.1176/ajp.152.11.1652. PMID: 7485630.

42. Spencer TJ, Faraone SV. Psychoactive substance use disorders in adults with attention deficit hyperactivity disorder (ADHD): effects of ADHD and psychiatric comorbidity. Am J Psychiatry. 1995 Nov;152(11):1652-8. doi: 10.1176/ajp.152.11.1652. PMID: 7485630.

43. Wilens TE, Biederman J, Mick E, Faraone SV, Spencer T. Attention deficit hyperactivity disorder (ADHD) is associated with early onset substance use disorders. J Nerv Ment Dis. 1997 Aug;185(8):475-82. doi: 10.1097/00005053-199708000-00001. PMID: 9284860.

44. Milberger S, Biederman J, Faraone SV, Wilens T, Chu MP. Associations between ADHD and psychoactive substance use disorders. Findings from a longitudinal study of high-risk siblings of ADHD children. Am J Addict. 1997 Fall;6(4):318-29. PMID: 9398930. DOI: 10.3109/10550499709005063

45. Timothy E. Wilens, Joseph Biederman & Eric Mick (1998) Does ADHD Affect the Course of Substance Abuse? Findings From a Sample of Adults With and Without ADHD, American Journal on Addictions, 7:2, 156-163. DOI: 10.3109/10550499809034487

46. SULLIVAN, M.A. and RUDNIK-LEVIN, F. (2001), Attention Deficit/Hyperactivity Disorder and Substance Abuse. Annals of the New York Academy of Sciences, 931: 251-270. https://doi.org/10.1111/j.1749-6632.2001.tb05783.x

47. Modesto-Lowe V, Chaplin M, Woodard K. Universal precautions to reduce stimulant misuse in treating adult ADHD. Cleveland Clinic Journal of Medicine August 2015, 82 (8) 506-512;

DOI: https://doi.org/10.3949/ccjm.82a.14131

48. Kessler RC, Adler L, Ames M, et al. The World Health Organization Adult ADHD Self-Report Scale (ASRS): a short screening scale for use in the general population. Psychol Med 2005; 35:245-256.

49. Kaye S, Darke S. The diversion and misuse of pharmaceutical stimu- lants: what do we know and why should we care? Addiction 2012; 107:467-477.

50. Novak SP, Kroutil LA, Williams RL, Van Brunt DL. The nonmedical use of prescription ADHD medications: results from a national Internet panel. Subst Abuse Treat Prev Policy 2007; 2:32.

51. Bavarian N, Flay BR, Ketcham P, et al. Using structural equation modeling to understand prescription stimulant misuse: a test of the Theory of Triadic Influence. Drug Alcohol Depend 2014; 138:193-201.

52. Volkow ND. Stimulant medications: how to minimize their reinforcing effects? Am J Psychiatry 2006; 163:359-361.

53. Kolar D, Keller A, Golfinopoulos M, Cumyn L, Syer C, Hechtman L. Treatment of adults with attention-deficit/hyperactivity disorder. Neuropsychiatr Dis Treat 2008; 4:107-121.

54. Schachter D, Tharmalingam S, Kleinman I. Informed consent and stimulant medication: adolescents' and parents' ability to understand information about benefits and risks of stimulant medication for the treatment of attention-deficit/hyperactivity disorder. J Child Adolesc Psychopharmacol 2011; 21:139-148.

55. Deep K. Use of narcotics contracts. Virtual Mentor 2013; 15:416–420.

56. Cheatle MD, Savage SR. Informed consent in opioid therapy: a potential obligation and opportunity. J Pain Symptom Manage 2012; 44:105–116.

57. Manning JS. Strategies for managing the risks associated with ADHD medications. J Clin Psychiatry 2013; 74:e19.

58. https://www.health.state.mn.us/communities/opioids/prevent ion/painperception.html#:~:text=The%20United%20States% 20makes%20up,80%25%20of%20the%20world's%20opioid s.

59. Manchikanti L., Singh A. Therapeutic opioids: a ten-year perspective on the complexities and complications of the escalating use, abuse, and nonmedical use of opioids) (Pain Physician 2008 Mar;11(2 Suppl):S63-88)

(References below are redundant at this time)

100. National Institute for Health and Care Excellence. Attention deficit hyperactivity disorder: diagnosis and management of ADHD in children, young people and adults. The British Psychological Society and The Royal College of Psychiatrists: United Kingdom; 2009.

101. Mannuzza S, Klein RG, Klein DF, Bessler A, Shrout P. Accuracy of adult recall of childhood attention deficit hyperactivity disorder. Am J Psychiatry 2002; 159:1882-1888.

102. Gittelman R, Mannuzza S, Shenker R, Bonagura N. Hyperactive boys almost grown up. I. Psychiatric status. Arch Gen Psychiatry. 1985 Oct;42(10):937-47. doi: 10.1001/archpsyc.1985.01790330017002. PMID: 4037987.)

Martin, N., Scourfield, J., & McGuffin, P. (2002). Observer effects and heritability of childhood attention-deficit hyperactivity disorder symptoms. *British Journal of Psychiatry, 180*(3), 260-265. doi:10.1192/bjp.180.3.260

Sherman, D. K., McGue, M. K., & Iacono, W. G. (1997). Twin concordance for attention deficit hyperactivity disorder: A comparison of teachers' and mothers' reports. *The American Journal of Psychiatry, 154*(4), 532-535. https://doi.org/10.1176/ajp.154.4.532

Ward, M. F., Wender, P. H., & Reimherr F. W. (1992). The Wender Utah rating scale: An aid in theretrospective diagnosis of childhood attention deficit hyperactivity disorder. *American Journal of Psychiatry, 150,* 885-888.

Zucker, M., Morris, M. K., Ingram, S. M., Morris, R. D., & Bakeman, R. (2002). Concordance of self- and informant ratings of adults' current and childhood attention-deficit/hyperactivity disorder symptoms.

Assessment and Treatment of ADHD with Addiction

(William Yvorchuk, MD CM)

The combination of an underlying ADHD condition beneath an active SUD presentation can be very difficult to determine correctly as the symptoms of active addiction, substance use followed by periods of withdrawal, often mimic the ADHD symptomatology. Ideally one would assess the ADHD condition once there has been a period of abstinence from illicit psychoactive substances. The achievement of abstinence in a timely fashion may be a difficult goal under most circumstances. The typical presentation of addiction to stimulant substances will often mask an underlying ADHD condition unless one is sensitive to the possibility of its presence. A high degree of vigilance is required to tease out the ADHD symptoms from the morass of behavioral aberrancies in consequence of a substantial SUD process. Furthermore, it is often unlikely that a provider treating a patient with active addiction or one early in recovery will consider prescribing pharmacologic grade stimulants without a firm diagnosis of ADHD because of the high propensity for misuse and abuse.

Patients with ADHD may have a particularly difficult time processing information and participating in group meetings due to their tendency for a high degree of impulsivity and acting out when not medically treated. Their dropout rate from formal recovery practice is, as a result, substantially higher as well.

Pharmacologic Agents:

A number of medications have been successfully employed in the treatment of ADHD. Both stimulant and some nonstimulant medications have had some success. The typical stimulant medications include the amphetamine analogs and methylphenidate. Nonstimulant medications include atomoxetine, bupropion, venlafaxine, tricyclic antidepressants, alpha-2 agonists and monoamine oxidase inhibitors, as well as Modafinil®. Modafinil® appears to be effective under some circumstances and may have a lower tendency for misuse.

Although the body of research on ADHD has expanded substantially over the last two decades, there is a paucity of studies on ADHD coupled with an active SUD condition.

One study (1) found that both formal stimulants and nonstimulant medications were superior to placebo control. A follow-up study reported that the stimulant medications remained superior to nonstimulants (2). These effects must be modulated with the appreciation that adults with ADHD tend to be less responsive to stimulant medications in treating their ADHD symptoms.

Some researchers and treatment providers are of the opinion that once the diagnosis of ADHD is made then the use of controlled substance level stimulants should be made available to the patient. As discussed in the previous chapters, pharmacologic-grade stimulants provide for emotional shifts in 'normal' (non-ADHD) adults that are particularly rewarding. The typical reward pathway response can be supra-physiologic. It is the response in the non-ADHD patient that may bring about the SUD condition.

The paradoxical response in the *true* ADHD patient to pharmaceutical grade stimulants appears to be protective and does not lead to the addicted condition.

Therefore, if the clinical provider who is faced with an addicted patient in whom ADHD is suspected, the quagmire lies in the element of uncertainty in accurately teasing out ADHD symptoms in a person with active addiction. If the patient actually has ADHD, their overall symptomatology may improve with the addition of the stimulant. If they do not improve, or worsen, one may think that the diagnosis of ADHD is incorrect and so withdraw the stimulant, when in fact it is the addiction that is driving the overall process. The great risk lies in providing stimulants for a patient suspected of ADHD and they do not actually have the condition and the overall condition worsens rapidly with the high risk of precipitating serious illness or demise in the patient.

As an overarching perspective, we need to remember that unlike the condition with most other substances of abuse, it is the normal (non-ADHD) response to pharmaceutical grade stimulants that is particularly rewarding, and thus conducive to the development of a physiologic dependence over time, and potentially to the development of a stimulant SUD. The paradoxical response to stimulants in the ADHD patient seems to be protective in the development of a SUD.

The childhood ADHD patient, who grows out of the condition as the brain matures and the prefrontal cortex begins to dampen the underlying subcortical structures, can develop into an adult who no longer has the condition functionally, but enjoys the emotional rewards from the chronic use of the stimulant and comes to rely on the physiologic benefits and continues to try to avoid the acute and post-acute withdrawal (PAW) symptoms as a result of the physiologic dependence after having been on the pharmaceutical stimulant for years. Such patients may be difficult to identify and particularly difficult to convince that their prescribed stimulant is no longer required.

In general, the overarching concern does not rest with the relatively few patients discussed above. Rather, the major concern is our culture's demand for immediate gratification through chemical means. It is the non-ADHD adult who feels their physiologic age and has had an opportunity to test the ingestion of a potent stimulant and enjoys the perceived physiologic benefits thereof. Multiple facets of their emotional and physiologic experience change, and they become convinced that they 'function better' under the influence of a potent stimulant.

This is no different than a patient who has suffered for decades after childhood trauma and consequent PTSD, who happens to find that the use of alcohol, a benzodiazepine or an opiate, can dramatically shift their internal emotional experience and become immediately convinced as well that they 'function better' under the influence of the chemical. The process is experientially similar in both situations. Immediate gratification of reward coupled with a marked emotional shift and an experiential movement toward a greater degree of perceived functionality.

The error of perception is the perceived need for a controlled substance to be ingested on a chronic basis for emotional modulation and a perceived improvement in function.

The unnecessary use of controlled substances for emotional modulation in our culture for immediate gratification, coupled with our emphasis on 'self', has led to the inordinate consumption of controlled substances in the US compared to all other countries.

According to the National Center for Drug Abuse Statistics (NCDAS) nearly 32 million Americans (11.7% of the population) were *actively* using drugs as of 2021. Marijuana, prescription stimulants and methamphetamines were the most popular drugs of choice (**3**)(**4**). This is a shocking statement given the explosion of opiate use in recent years.

According to a recent study assessing the use of stimulants in the general US population (**5**), "Amphetamine use increased 2.5-fold from 2006 to 2016". "Total stimulant usage doubled in the last decade. There were dynamic changes but also regional disparities in the use of stimulant medications."

NIH recently reviewed the problem and published a report (**6**) revised June 2020 on the 'Misuse of Prescription Drugs (Research Report)'.

The following information was based on a NSDUH 2020 report (**7**).

Among people aged 12 or older in 2020:

- 5.8% (or about 16.1 million people) reported misusing any prescription psychotherapeutic drug in the past 12 months.
- 1.8% (or about 5.1 million people) reported misusing prescription stimulants in the past 12 months.
- 2.2% (or about 6.2 million people) reported misusing prescription tranquilizers or sedatives in the past 12 months.
- 1.7% (or about 4.8 million people) reported misusing benzodiazepines in the past 12 months.
- 3.3% (or about 9.3 million people) reported misusing prescription pain relievers in the past 12 months.

The following information was based on a Monitoring the Future Survey 2021 (**8**).

Among young people in 2021:

- An estimated 4.4% of 12th graders reported misusing any prescription drug in the past 12 months
- An estimated 3.0% of 8th graders, 2.7% of 10th graders, and 2.3% of 12th graders reported misusing amphetamines in the past 12 months
- An estimated 0.6% of 8th graders, 0.3% of 10th graders, and 0.5% of 12th graders reported misusing Ritalin in the past 12 months.
- An estimated 1.8% of 8th graders, 1.6% of 10th graders, and 1.8% of 12th graders reported misusing Adderall in the past 12 months
- An estimated 1.8% of 12th graders reported misusing sedatives (barbiturates) in the past 12 months

- An estimated 1.1% of 8th graders, 1.3% of 10th graders, and 1.2% of 12th graders reported misusing tranquilizers in the past 12 months
- An estimated 1.0% of 12th graders reported misusing narcotics other than heroin in the past 12 months
- An estimated 0.8% of 8th graders, 0.9% of 10th graders, and 0.9% of 12th graders reported misusing OxyContin in the past 12 months
- An estimated 0.6% of 8th graders, 0.5% of 10th graders, and 0.9% of 12th graders reported misusing Vicodin in the past 12 months

Among people aged 12 or older in 2020, an estimated 0.3% (or about 758,000 people) had a prescription stimulant use disorder in the past 12 months (**9**).

Approximately 80% of the global opioid supply is consumed in the United States with 99% of the world's supply of hydrocodone (**10**).

There is a question as to whether there is an overdiagnosis of ADHD in the US (**11**). Per the report "ADHD is known as an American disorder because of the high prevalence and number of cases in the country. In 2014, the ADHD prevalence in the US for ages 3 years and older was 6.91%, while the 5EU combined and Japan only had prevalence estimates of 1.23% and 1.21%, respectively." "Additionally, the number of cases of ADHD in the US accounted for 80.0% of all ADHD cases in the 7MM (US, 5EU, and Japan) in 2014. We expect this pattern to continue into the next decade, with the number of cases in the US accounting for 84.5% of ADHD cases in the 7MM in 2024."

A systematic review study published recently (**12**) attempted to review all literature on the non-medical use (NMU) and diversion of prescription stimulants. They were able to review some 111 studies on the topic. One of the findings resulting from the analysis was " A total of 111 studies met inclusion criteria. NMU and diversion of stimulants are *highly prevalent*; self-reported rates among population samples range from 2.1% to 58.7% and from 0.7% to 80.0%, respectively." Furthermore, "NMU of stimulants is a significant public health problem, especially in college students, but variations in the terms used to describe NMU and inconsistencies in the available data limit a better understanding of this problem".

A recent study (**13**) looking at the trends in use of prescription stimulants in the US reports that "The US accounts for **<5%** of the world's population but **83.1%** of the global volume of ADHD medications (**14**)." (bold added)

This is an astounding finding because this statistic stands in stark contrast with the premise that ADHD is a behavioral disorder common to children worldwide.

A study focused on the prevalence of ADHD worldwide (**15**) reviewed some 50 studies of which 20 were studies in US populations and 30 were in non-US populations. The discussion centers on opposing perspectives that on one hand the predominance of American research "led to the impression that ADHD is largely an American disorder and is much less prevalent elsewhere. This impression was reinforced by the perception that ADHD may stem from social and cultural factors that are most common in American society." This is opposed by another school of thought that "ADHD is a behavioral disorder common to children of many different races and societies worldwide, but that is not recognized by the medical community, perhaps due to confusion regarding its diagnosis and/or misconceptions regarding its adverse impact on children, their families, and society as a whole."

The results of the global study reviews according to the authors report that "Analysis of these studies suggests that the prevalence of ADHD is at least as high in many non-US children as in US children, with the highest prevalence rates being seen when using DSM-IV diagnoses. Recognition that ADHD is not purely an American disorder and that the prevalence of this behavioral disorder in many countries is in the *same range as that in the USA* will have important implications for the psychiatric care of children." (Italics placed by this author)

The important takeaway is that despite the apparent similarity in prevalence of ADHD worldwide, the US consumes over 80% of the world's supply of stimulants.

It becomes clear that the population in this country ingests more controlled substance stimulants than required for medically and functionally based reasons.

Time will tell whether the way of the stimulant epidemic will follow the trajectory of the recent opioid epidemic and its serious consequences.

Nonmedical Use of Psychoactive Stimulants:

Nonmedical use of prescribed medication (diversion of a controlled substance) includes the use of any controlled substance outside of the specific directives on the prescription. These can include taking more than prescribed, transferring to someone who does not have a prescription for same such as selling, trading or simply giving it away, as well as combining the prescribed substance with alcohol or other illicit psychoactive substances.

Approximately 0.6% of Americans 12 yr. or older report last 30 day (current) nonmedical use of stimulants. The rate for nonmedical use of opioids is nearly triple at 1.6%.

Rates of misuse of stimulant medications hovers around 5 to 10% of high school students and peaks in range from 5% to 35% among college students (16). The issue is compounded when one considers that approximately 31% of college students prescribed stimulants misused their medication with intranasal use in 8% within the previous 6 months as well as diversion to peers in 26% (17). The prime consideration in misuse was performance enhancement. Complicating factors that increase the risk of stimulant misuse include excess use of alcohol with binge drinking in this population as well as the propensity for using other illicit chemicals as well.

The risk of illicit use, including diversion, appears to be nearly twice as high with patients prescribed stimulants as compared to patient prescribed controlled substances such as opioids for chronic nonmalignant pain (CNMP), benzodiazepines and Z-drugs for insomnia and anxiety (18).

One study revealed that students may seek help for ADHD after they self-diagnose after the discovery that stimulants diverted from colleagues improved their concentration (19). One problem is that over 40% of students in the group admitted to still using stimulants to 'get high'. A confounding issue is that stimulants help with energy, focus and concentration in normal subjects, those without diagnosable ADHD. There appears to be a narrow margin between therapeutic use and misuse and abuse of stimulant medications.

Differing formulations and delivery systems for some of the stimulant medications offer a delayed release of the substance along with a sustained delivery of medication over time. One advantage was found that there is substantially less abuse liability with these formulations and may be helpful in patients with co-occurring addiction (20)(21)(22). The subjective effects of long-acting agents are associated with less positive stimulant euphorigenic effects.

The issue of conduct disorder with ADHD leads to a greater degree of behavioral 'acting out' and is coupled with a greater degree of SUD and medication abuse with immediate-release rather than extended-release formulations (23).

Overuse of potent stimulants carries potential complications such as serious hypertension and cardiovascular events such as arrythmia, cardiac ischemia, and cerebral ischemic events. Unsupervised excess use of stimulants is fraught with medical complications particularly as age increases. Such medical conditions can also be precipitated through unfavorable interactions with other prescription medication as well as the use of unregulated over-the-counter medications.

Non-Stimulant Medications:

Atomoxetine and guanfacine extended-release have been found to be of some benefit in the treatment of ADHD and appear to have lower abuse potential than traditional stimulants in patients also suffering from SUD.

Atomoxetine is a centrally acting noradrenergic reuptake inhibitor (24). It effectively increases the availability of norepinephrine as a neurotransmitter thus acting as a muted stimulant. It is not traditionally a medication that has much in terms of abuse potential. It may take a few weeks for the medication to take effect much in the same manner as serotonergic antidepressants in the treatment of clinical depression.

Guanfacine (extended-release) is a centrally acting alpha 2 agonist that appears to be nearly as effective as traditional stimulants in younger patients (25). This medication appears to have little abuse potential.

Clonidine is another noradrenergic alpha 2 agonist medication with some efficacy in treating ADHD (**26**).

Some other antidepressant substances have some value in treating ADHD with little abuse potential. Bupropion, a do-paminergic antidepressant with norepinephrine reuptake inhibition properties, widely used in the treatment of depression has had some efficacy in treating ADHD and is coupled with little abuse potential making it a safer option in treating patients with SUDs (27)(28). Venlafaxine, a norepinephrine-serotonin reuptake inhibitor (NSRI), is also widely used for the treatment of clinical depression, has some limited efficacy in treating ADHD and is again a safer option when also treating a patient with substance use disorder (29)(30). Tricyclic antidepressants (TCA), such as desipramine, block the reuptake of norepinephrine in the synaptic cleft making more available as a neurotransmitter. These medications have some efficacy in treating ADHD and can be used with some safety in SUD patients (31). Monoamine oxidase inhibitors can also be effective in treating ADHD but these medications can lead to hypertensive crises in association with tyramine-containing foods (various cheeses; cured, smoked or processed meats; pickled vegetables; fermented soy products). The use of MAOIs can have serious medical consequences and overuse can be life threatening. These medications are contraindicated in patients with SUDs.

The therapeutic use of stimulant medications, albeit more effective in treating ADHD, can be quite problematic in the SUD population. To date the few studies that have addressed their use in the ADHD-SUD population reveal mixed results in efficacy of treatment (32)(33)(34)(35)(36)(37)(38). Mixed results may result from a confluence of factors such as continued illicit substance use leading to less responsiveness to the treating medication, poor adherence to the medication trial, inadequate dosing, difficulty in diagnosis, coexistent morbidities.

Nonmedication Options for ADHD with SUD:

There is less data for nonpharmacologic approaches to the treatment of ADHD coupled with SUD. As in the treatment of SUD patients with other comorbidities, addressing both the ADHD and SUD disorders concurrently provides an improved benefit compared to treating either alone.

Traditional types of psychotherapeutic interventions include cognitive behavioral therapy (CBT), behavior modification (BM), relapse prevention techniques, psychoeducation and twelve-step facilitation (TSF). Meditation and mindfulness training provide another venue for emotional modulation practice. The combination of medication and psychotherapeutic modalities offer a greater degree of recovery than either alone (39)(40)(41).

(Adapted from Addiction Medicine 6th Ed)

A Proposal for the Treatment of Addiction in General:

In a previous chapter, we reviewed a perspective on the nature of Addiction as a disease based on aberrancies in the meso-cortical limbic system perturbations from the use of excessive amounts of psychotropic medication in a fashion that behavior appears to be out of control with an inability to stop use of the substance(s) despite negative consequences.

We have also considered the personal perspective of perceiving Addiction as the experience of a profound emotional disease based on chronic attachment to suffering and victimization.

In that light, we propose an alternate holistic approach to the treatment of a SUD that dovetails seamlessly with other traditional practices for the improvement of Addiction.

The emphasis is a practice of emotional recovery on a daily basis which is congruent with the currently available methods, pharmacologic, holistic and otherwise.

We read that our true emotional baseline resides in that 'peace that surpasses understanding' arising from our original experiential state, which can most simply be described as:

No 'me' - No mind - No time

As we all begin this life's journey with the experience beyond 'self' and thus beyond thought, there is no sense of time. We only experience the present moment without any experience of self (me) or time. This is a universal experience regardless of our heredity or heritage; regardless of nature or nurture.

Every one of us born into this world comes into it with the same underlying experience of - 'no me, no mind, no time'.

One reason that drugs of abuse are so difficult to forego is that they become the chemical 'key to the lock' of our emotional nervous system. They become the most efficient and rapid means to experientially shift us from the emotional distress experienced within ourselves to that freedom from ourselves and toward our universal baseline state of *experiential* peace.

The next observation that arises is: if we can move toward this universal baseline state of freedom from self with a profoundly quiet mind, and thus with a vast reduction in the sense of time without the use of substances of abuse, then we should not need them for our experiential recovery.

A simple observation is that in the vast majority of circumstances 'everything is fine right here and right now'.

If we can be freed from our underlying, stored, emotional baggage, then we are at a much greater advantage to release drugs of abuse.

It is well recognized that addiction is a disorder at the bi-opsychosocial level of functioning. In essence, addiction invades and corrupts all aspects of daily life on a personal and relationship (including familial) level.

Consistent with a proposal offered to a major University the following parameters are presented below.

Objective: Improvement in the efficiency of resolving the fundamental resistance to *emotional recovery* from Addiction

Challenges

- Requirement of paradigm shift in focusing on the degree òf self-identification as a measure of emotional health
- The paradigm includes an assessment of the degree of attachment through self to emotional suffering and the experience of victimization

- Development of an experiential program addressing relief from the emotional distress of addiction and extending to the emotional duress of everyday life
- Transcending preconscious barriers to emotional release and thus toward emotional freedom
- Motivation toward Daily Commitment to a path of Experiential Recovery
- Prejudice against a Higher Power – an 'Infinite Organizing Force' of the Universe

Limitations that cause problem to exist

- Perception that the solution to addiction is primarily pharmacologic (Bio) and based in CBT (including relapse prevention) and Behavior Modification (Psycho-Social) without addressing the pervasive, ongoing, emotional distress that promotes recurrent substance use
- Misperception that the spiritual component of the traditional 12-Step recovery program involves a similar path
- Misunderstanding with respect to our Baseline Emotional State
- Lack of appreciation that the application of self-will actually limits emotional recovery
- Lack of appreciation that the application of self-will cannot truly provide for genuine, stable emotional recovery that can withstand duress
- Appreciation that Addiction is a Brain Disease coupled with possible lack of appreciation that it has a profound emotional underpinning that can be radically modified

- Lack of appreciation that an experiential approach may provide an emotional solution to the Addiction issue

Proposed solution

- To have patients embark on a path of recovery that is based in evidenced-based addiction medicine principles with the addition of a systematized experiential approach to surrendering attachments to emotional burdens and thus move toward the experience of – no 'self; profoundly quiet mind; no time (only now)
- Dovetails with meditation practice, mindfulness practice; with the addition of a path toward radical forgiveness of everyone for everything, along with a complete surrender of victimhood, thus fostering a return toward experiential innocence – our true baseline emotional state

Barriers to success

- Begin with the requirement for a shift in mindset with respect to the approach in addiction treatment from pharmacology and cognitive – social rehabilitation to allow for the acceptance of an emotional – experiential approach as the basis for emotional change and the profound emotional attachment to drugs of abuse

Benefits

- Patients suffering from addiction would benefit from an experiential approach that allows for a more profound and complete emotional recovery with substantially lowered risk of relapse and a radically renewed relationship with their families, friends and acquaintances
- Each patient stands to benefit from the addiction issue along with a major benefit to daily living through the experience of freedom from the emotionally burdened 'self' which should translate into a radical shift in the experiential relationship with the world and everyone in it
- Patients experience marked improvement in emotional – experiential recovery
- Once a manualized process of experiential emotional recovery is established and refined within the addiction problem (emotions, and thus behavior, out of control); it can be expanded to other neuroses such as moderate and severe depression and anxiety, and the like

Milestones

- Baseline and periodic re-evaluation through standard emotional testing
- Assessment of recovery participation
- Assessment of objective parameters (urine testing; meeting participation; progress through experiential 'step' work)
- Documented improvement in nature of relationships; familial, at work and social

References:

1. Torgersen T, Gjervan B, Rasmussen K. Treatment of adult ADHD: is current knowledge useful to clinicians? *Neuropsychiatr Dis Treat.* 2008;4(1):177-186.

2. Faraone SV, Glatt SJ. A comparison of the efficacy of medications for adult attention-deficit/hyperactivity disorder using meta-analysis of effect sizes. *J Clin Psychiatry.* 2010;71(6):754-763.

3. https://drugabusestatistics.org/

4. https://www.kolmac.com/why-is-drug-use-in-america-on-the-rise/

5. Piper BJ, Ogden CL, Simoyan OM, Chung DY, Caggiano JF, Nichols SD, et al. (2018) Trends in use of prescription stimulants in the United States and Territories, 2006 to 2016. PLoS ONE 13 (11): e0206100. https://doi.org/10.1371/journal. pone.0206100

6. NIH Research Report; Revised June 2020; Misuse of Prescription Drugs Research Report

7. https://www.samhsa.gov/data/release/2020-national-survey-drug-use-and-health-nsduh-releases

8. http://www.monitoringthefuture.org/data/data.html

   https://nida.nih.gov/drug-topics/trends-statistics/infographics/monitoring-future-2021-survey-results

9. 2020 National Survey on Drug Use and Health

   https://www.samhsa.gov/data/release/2020-national-survey-drug-use-and-health-nsduh-releases

10. https://www.cnbc.com/2016/04/27/americans-consume-almost-all-of-the-global-opioid-supply.html#:~:text=Americans%20are%20in%20more%20pain,consumed%20in%20the%20United%20States.

11. Global Data

    https://www.pharmaceutical-technology.com/marketdata/commentis-adhd-an-american-disorder-5726770/#:~:text=ADHD%20is%20known%20as%20an,%2C%20respectively%20(Figure%201)

12. Faraone SV, Rostain AL, Montano CB, Mason O, Antshel KM, Newcorn JH. Systematic Review: Nonmedical Use of Prescription Stimulants: Risk Factors, Outcomes, and Risk Reduction Strategies. J Am Acad Child Adolesc Psychiatry. 2020 Jan;59(1):100-112. doi: 10.1016/j.jaac.2019.06.012. Epub 2019 Jul 19. PMID: 31326580.

13. Piper BJ, Ogden CL, Simoyan OM, et al. Trends in use of prescription stimulants in the United States and Territories, 2006 to 2016. PLoS One. 2018;13(11):e0206100. Published 2018 Nov 28. doi:10.1371/journal.pone.0206100

14. Scheffler RM, Hinshaw SP, Modrek S, et al. The global market for ADHD medications. Health Affairs. 2007; 26:450–457.

https://doi.org/10.1377/hlthaff.26.2.450 PMID: 17339673

15. Faraone SV, Sergeant J, Gillberg C, Biederman J. The worldwide prevalence of ADHD: is it an American condition? World Psychiatry. 2003 Jun;2(2):104-13. PMID: 16946911; PMCID: PMC1525089.

16. Clemow DB, Walker DJ. The potential for misuse and abuse of medications in ADHD: a review. Postgrad Med. 2014;126(5):64-81.

17. McCabe SE, et al. Non-medical use of prescription stimulants among US college students: prevalence and correlates from a national survey. Addiction. 2005;100(1):96-106.

18. Rabiner DL, et al. The misuse and diversion of prescribed ADHD medications by college students. J Atten Disord. 2009;13(2):144-153.

19. Rostain AL, Ramsay JR. A combined treatment approach for adults with ADHD—results of an open study of 43 patients. J Atten Disord. 2006;10(2):150-159.

20. Findling RL. Evolution of the treatment of attention-deficit/hyperactivity disorder in children: a review. Clin Ther. 2008;30(5):942-957.

21. Mao AR, Babcock T, Brams M. ADHD in adults: current treatment trends with consideration of abuse potential of medications. J Psychiatr Pract. 2011;17(4):241-250.

22. Mariani JJ, Levin FR. Psychostimulant treatment of cocaine dependence. Psychiatr Clin North Am. 2012;35(2):425-439.

23. Wilens TE, et al. Characteristics of adolescents and young adults with ADHD who divert or misuse their prescribed medications. J Am Acad Child Adolesc Psychiatry. 2006;45(4):408-414.

24. Adler LA, et al. Long-term, open-label study of the safety and efficacy of atomoxetine in adults with attention-deficit/hyperactivity disorder: an interim analysis. J Clin Psychiatry. 2005;66(3):294-299.

25. Faraone SV, Buitelaar J. Comparing the efficacy of stimulants for ADHD in children and adolescents using meta-analysis. Eur Child Adolesc Psychiatry. 2010;19(4):353-364.

26. Faraone SV, Glatt SJ. A comparison of the efficacy of medications for adult attention-deficit/hyperactivity disorder using meta-analysis of effect sizes. J Clin Psychiatry. 2010;71(6):754-763.

27. Conners CK, et al. Bupropion hydrochloride in attention deficit disorder with hyperactivity. J Am Acad Child Adolesc Psychiatry. 1996;35(10):1314-1321.

28. Wilens TE, et al. A controlled clinical trial of bupropion for attention deficit hyperactivity disorder in adults. Am J Psychiatry. 2001;158(2):282-288.

29. Olvera RL, et al. An open trial of venlafaxine in the treatment of attention-deficit/hyperactivity disorder in children and adolescents. J Child Adolesc Psychopharmacol. 1996;6(4):241-250.

30. Amiri S, et al. Double-blind controlled trial of venlafaxine for treatment of adults with attention deficit/hyperactivity disorder. Hum Psychopharmacol. 2012;27(1):76-81.

31. Wolraich ML, et al. Attention-deficit/hyperactivity disorder among adolescents: a review of the diagnosis, treatment, and clinical implications. Pediatrics. 2005;115(6):1734-1746.

32. Levin FR, et al. Treatment of cocaine dependent treatment seekers with adult ADHD: double-blind comparison of methylphenidate and placebo. Drug Alcohol Depend. 2007;87(1):20-29.

33. Schubiner H, Saules KK, Arfken CL, et al. Double-blind placebo-controlled trial of methylphenidate in the treatment of adult ADHD patients with comorbid cocaine dependence. Exp Clin Psychopharmacol. 2002 Aug;10(3):286-294.

34. Carpentier PJ, de Jong CA, Dijkstra BA, Verbrugge CA, Krabbe PF. A controlled trial of methylphenidate in adults with attention deficit/hyperactivity disorder and substance use disorders. Addiction. 2005;100(12):1868-1874.

35. Levin FR, Evans SM, Brooks DJ, Kalbag AS, Garawi F, Nunes EV.Treatment of methadone-maintained patients with adult ADHD: double-blind comparison of methylphenidate, bupropion and placebo. Drug Alcohol Depend. 2006;81(2):137-148.

36. Konstenius M, et al. Sustained release methylphenidate for the treatment of ADHD in amphetamine abusers: a pilot study. Drug Alcohol Depend. 2010;108(1-2):130-133.

37. Konstenius M, et al. Methylphenidate for attention deficit hyperactivity disorder and drug relapse in criminal offenders with substance dependence: a 24-week randomized placebo-controlled trial. Addiction. 2014;109(3):440-449.

38. Levin FR, et al. Extended-release mixed amphetamine salts vs placebo for comorbid adult attention-deficit/hyperactivity disorder and cocaine use disorder: a Randomized Clinical

39. March JS, et al. Anxiety as a predictor and outcome variable in the multimodal treatment study of children with ADHD (MTA). J Abnorm Child Psychol. 2000;28(6):527-541.

40. Safren SA, et al. Cognitive behavioral therapy vs relaxation with educational support for medication-treated adults with ADHD and persistent symptoms: a randomized controlled trial. JAMA. 2010;304(8):875-880.

41. Philipsen A. Psychotherapy in adult attention deficit hyperactivity disorder: implications for treatment and research. Expert Rev Neurother. 2012;12(10):1217-1225.

⑨

What Do We Do Now?

(Wayne Lewis Creelman, MD)

Now that the reader has had an opportunity to become much more knowledgeable regarding the diagnosis and treatment of ADHD, what are the bottom-line take home messages from this expose of the ADHD disorder.

ADHD is an impairment of a complex syndrome of brain functions that are essential for successful and lifelong self-management. Those individuals who suffer the pathology have a difficulty typically getting motivated, organized and are just not self-starters. It is a complex syndrome, or rather, a cluster of impairments better renamed as an "executive function deficit disorder". This is because it is a developmental impairment of executive functions. It effects children, adolescents and adults in the executive functions of organizing the day, focusing on tasks during the day, sustaining effort to complete the tasks, modulating one's emotions while completing the tasks, using working memory in a successful fashion and finally performing actions that bring closure to challenges and jobs that need to be done.

The primary problem of ADHD is that of a lack of attention. Because of the increasing demand today for academic achievement in youngsters regarding educational efforts and in adults with the expectation for enhanced work performance, it is too easy to assume that the individual is suffering ADHD when poor grades occur in school or the adult's inability to advance in one's company, when reality is simply - under achievement. It is clear that in childhood and adolescence boys out number Girls with close to a 3 to 1 ratio. In adults the ratio is closer to 1 to 1, as the childhood differential may be due to the fact that girls in general tend to be less disruptive in the classroom with teachers or at home with parents where there are boy counterparts. With adults there has become increased recognition that women also struggle with the syndrome in a ratio almost identical to men.

One of the challenges in making the diagnosis and then allowing treatment to minimize the dysfunction is that everyone has ADHD symptoms at times. The difference between the average person and one suffering ADHD is in the severity of impairment. Those suffering the pathology have more persistent and chronic symptoms that reduce their quality of life. The symptoms are more impairing and the patient's lifestyle is seriously impaired by the symptoms. In those with ADHD there typically exists serious impairment with many aspects of daily living. But the pathology is not an all-or-nothing illness like pregnancy. For decades it has been postulated that ADHD starts in childhood.

But it is clear from a variety of studies that some individuals begin to develop impairments in midlife with the symptoms becoming expressed when significant lifecycle challenges occur. It is also clear from research that ADHD impairments persist into adulthood, generally not so much with the hyperactivity but more so with the inattentiveness. It is also clear from research that 75 percent of individuals with

ADHD in childhood will continue to experience significant ADHD-related impairments into adulthood. Longitudinal studies have shown that approximately 70 percent of individuals will have some impairments through the life span when diagnosed in childhood. It is also clear that ADHD symptoms are found in individuals across the full range of intellectual abilities. ADHD is not a problem of reduced IQ.

ADHD is highly inheritable. Individuals with the pathology demonstrate a 2 to 3-year delay in the development of certain areas of the brain with the thickening of the cortex of the brain's gray matter lagging behind their peers without the pathology. There is also a slow development of efficient circuitry of the brain with the white matter and a slowed transit of neural signals below the surface of the cortex. ADHD runs in families with 25 percent of children with ADHD having had a parent with ADHD and 30 percent having a brother or sister with the pathology. However, what is inherited is the vulnerability to the disorder. This is not an issue of eye color genetics.

Another phenomenon that has been recognized is that most medical and mental health professionals have had very little or no professional training in the assessment or treatment of ADHD. Thus, determining whether a child, adolescent or adult has ADHD with a reduction in executive functions significantly underdeveloped relative to those of most individuals of comparable age, is a challenge of professional proportions. ADHD is not positively or negatively correlated with IQ but rather the brain's central processing system. Additional life stresses can become overwhelming and cause the expression of symptoms in an otherwise non-affected individual. A meta-analysis of 102 studies including over 170,000 individuals found the prevalence of ADHD to be in the ballpark of 5.3 percent with those adolescents 18 years or younger from all regions of the world. The percentage of Americans with the disorder is an aberration of the global statistics.

There is also enormous contradictory information in the public forum, in the media and on the Internet regarding ADHD. Much of the information is unscientific, outdated or simply wrong. No biological marker exists to make the diagnosis of ADHD as it is a functional problem. Unfortunately, long-term studies show that those individuals with ADHD are less likely to complete high school, complete less post high school education, are less likely to complete a college degree, are more likely to be employed in unskilled occupations, are more likely to have a substance abuse disorder, are more likely to quit or be fired from a job, are at an increased risk of premature death (mostly due to accidents) and one study indicated an elevated risk for attempted and completed suicide.

For those individuals with ADHD, 80 percent of children, adolescents and adults benefit greatly from medication intervention. At the same time, most children, adolescents and adults who have ADHD also have comorbidity with one or more additional learning or psychiatric disorders at some point in their lives. These include learning disabilities, conduct disorders, anxiety disorders, depressive disorders as well as autism spectrum disorders.

This text has walked the reader through the importance of making an accurate diagnosis of the disorder in order to implement successful treatment and minimize the dysfunctions recognized in the untreated individual with the pathology. At the same time, those individuals without the pathology clearly have an increased risk of morbidity with unnecessary use of psychostimulant medication leading to problems of addiction and dependency on controlled medications indefinitely without professional intervention. We see this problem every day in our center with multiple patient's expressing "don't take away my Adderall" during first time evaluations. Let those who have ears listen to the caution of inaccurate diagnoses and unnecessary prescription of addictive stimulant medication with the multiple morbidities that follow lazy assessment and frivolous treatment.

Author Biographies

Dr. Creelman is the McCabe Professor of Psychiatry at the University of Florida, board-certified in general psychiatry and a national expert in community psychiatry and psychopharmacology. He trained at Boston College, Georgetown School of Medicine and Tulane School of Public Health.

Dr. Sang Koo is an assistant professor of psychiatry at the University of Florida Department of Psychiatry, board-certified in child and adult psychiatry and completed a prestigious fellowship in Child and Adolescent Psychiatry at the Washington University School of Medicine in Saint Louis Missouri.

Dr. William Yvorchuk is an assistant professor in the Department of Psychiatry at the University of Florida, the medical director of Addiction Medicine at the Vero Beach Center for Psychiatry and Addiction Medicine, completed a fellowship in Addiction Medicine at the University of Florida College of Medicine and is certified in Addiction Medicine by the American Board of addiction medicine. He is also a diplomate of the American Board of Preventive Medicine.